הַגָּדָה שֶׁל פֶּסַח

A PASSOVER HAGGADAH

הגדה של פסח

והגדת לבנך ביום ההוא לאמר

A PASSOVER HAGGADAH

Second Revised Edition

"As it is said: You shall tell your child on that day"

The New Union Haggadah Edited by Herbert Bronstein for the Central Conference of American Rabbis

Drawings by Leonard Baskin

The Viking Press New York

Penguin Books Ltd, Harmondsworth, Middlesex, England
Penguin Books, 625 Madison Avenue, New York, New York 10022, U.S.A.
Penguin Books Australia Ltd, Ringwood, Victoria, Australia
Penguin Books Canada Limited, 2801 John Street, Markham, Ontario, Canada L3R 1B4
Penguin Books (N.Z.) Ltd, 182–190 Wairau Road, Auckland 10, New Zealand

First published in the United States of America
in simultaneous hardcover and paperback editions
by Grossman Publishers and the Central Conference of American Rabbis 1974
Revised edition published by the Central Conference of American Rabbis 1975
Published in Penguin Books 1978
Second revised edition published by
the Central Conference of American Rabbis
and in Penguin Books 1982

Copyright © Central Conference of American Rabbis, 1974, 1975, 1982
All rights reserved

ISBN 0-670-54188-5

Printed in the United States of America

Liturgy Committee of the Central Conference of American Rabbis
Robert I. Kahn, Chairman 1967–1973
A. Stanley Dreyfus, Chairman 1973–
Herbert Bronstein — Richard N. Levy
A. Stanley Dreyfus — Eugene Mihaly
Harvey J. Fields — Joseph R. Narot
Albert A. Goldman — Nathan A. Perilman
Leonard S. Kravitz — Chaim Stern
Dudley Weinberg
Herbert Bronstein, Editor of the Haggadah
Joseph B. Glaser, *ex-officio* — Jack Bemporad, *ex-officio*
Malcolm H. Stern, *ex-officio* — Sidney L. Regner, *ex-officio*
Edward Graham, for the American Conference of Cantors
Tom Freudenheim, Chairman of the Art Advisory Committee

The pagination of this revised edition corresponds to the pagination of the original editon so that both editions may be used interchangeably.

Page 123 constitutes an extension of this copyright page.

Except in the United States of America,
this book is sold subject to the condition
that it shall not, by way of trade or otherwise,
be lent, re-sold, hired out, or otherwise circulated
without the publisher's prior consent in any form of
binding or cover other than that in which it is
published and without a similar condition
including this condition being imposed
on the subsequent purchaser

PREFACE

The Seder, the ceremonial feast of Passover, is an incomparable religious creation. It represents the unique artistry of the Jewish soul. The Liturgy Committee of the Central Conference of American Rabbis hoped to prepare a Haggadah that would have the power to summon up for our time the Seder's potency of joy and meaning. Before such a task, one must feel like the artisan called upon to fashion the wondrous staff of our first teacher, Moses, through whom the Redeemer of Israel worked signs and marvels in the land of Egypt. No matter how small, every strand should be strong and worthy in that miraculous interweaving of life, the שלשלת הקבלה, the great bond of our tradition.

And so the first stage in the preparation of this text was a study of the original creative impulses that brought the Seder into being; its earliest sources, structure, and motifs; as well as its development over the centuries. The convictions derived from that original process of study determined the philosophy underlying this Haggadah. Through the years of creative discussion and arduous labor on the part of the Liturgy Committee, those principles have remained intact.

Over the generations, the clarity of the Seder's classic form was blurred and even marred through changes or interpretations of the text of the Haggadah as the generations responded to the demands of immediate historic circumstances. One example will suffice: At some point, an original opening thematic statement of the Haggadah, "A fugitive Aramean was my father," was transformed into a polemic against a contemporaneous Syrian foe, and the text was translated, "An Aramean sought to destroy my father." Our own historic perspective, and our freedom to break with strict adherence to the text handed down to us from late medieval times, enable us to engage in a work of restoration. Indeed, one purpose (though not the only one) of this Haggadah is to allow the genius of the original to speak to us again; to permit the discovery of patterns and designs in the texture of the liturgy itself without undue didactic pointing.

So this Haggadah is not a revision of the previous Union Haggadah. It is an attempt at *renovatio ab origine*: a return to the creative beginning so as to bring forth what is utterly new from what was present in the old. Throughout, we have endeavored to be faithful to the elemental structure of the Haggadah, be-

ginning with the statement of the theme—the movement from degradation to glory—and the intentional complement of the story of Israel's own deliverance with the Messianic vision for all humanity.

In the struggle to express spiritual truth, religious genius has always had to make do with the language of flesh and blood derived from physical, material reality. Thus religious statements are almost always best made in myth and symbol and image; in sum, through metaphor, in likenesses and parables. To take such statements literally, we know, is to miss many levels of their meaning, if not to misunderstand them entirely. Though for many it is a present physical longing, the statement "Next year in Jerusalem!" far transcends the actuality of present geographical aspirations. It speaks also in the mode of our mystics, of ירושלים של מעלה, *Yerushalayim shel maalah*, of the homecoming of all existence, even of the Divine. In short, our approach to the language of the Haggadah has not been constricted or entrapped by the literalistic, the crude and heavy fence of an overly rationalistic literalism which in the past was often set around the gardens of our liturgy, and which sometimes fell in and smashed the flowers.

Every religious symbol is rooted in heaven, like the burning bush never consumed, though continuously alight with inexhaustible meaning. So the effort has been made to preserve intact those symbols and images that form our dream of redemption, to guard against willful semantic depletion of our symbols, and especially to fend off the reduction of their meanings to that narrow band of the spectrum of illumination that our limited perspective permits us to see. The Elijah passage represents one attempt to preserve this sense of reverence before the mysterious pluralities of the transcendent.

An authentic Seder experience is a process of the regeneration of values. More, it is the living experience of redemption. And the Haggadah is the accompaniment.

It is not intended that this Haggadah provide a series of inspirational preachments or intellectual discourses. It is hoped rather that the Haggadah will be a gateway to the actual experience of redemption, new and different each year, yet ever permanent in the realities of our history and ever reluming our vision of life. Nor did we want to provide commentary and opinion on current issues and events. For example, we had to fight the temptation of yet another presentation of "The Four Sons," gotten up in the trappings of current ideology to play parts in the debate on modern Jewish identity.

So we have striven for the archetypal rather than the current reference, for the allusive and suggestive rather than the didactic and explicit. Poetry and prose already endowed with the authority of durability speak to our present preoccupations far better than could an explicit current reference; and the Holocaust and the modern Jewish national rebirth find their place in this Haggadah because the tragedy and exaltation of our historic existence have already provided a place for them within the Seder, this story of our life whose shining conclusion is yet to unfold.

In this Haggadah, most of the rubrics of the traditional Haggadah are retained.

The leader of the Seder can choose to keep the original placement of the eating of the ceremonial *matzah* and *maror*. But even the new placement (suggested in the interest of a worthy and unhurried Seder) has a basis in ancient procedure: In ancient times, the eating of the ceremonial foods took place earlier in the Seder.

To cite another example: The *Hallel* psalms, perhaps the earliest element in ancient Passover worship, are retained. But the psalms themselves do not appear in their original form. The attempt has been made, rather, in our reordering of those texts, to reveal to ordinary gaze the overarching theme of those religious poems: the affirmation and triumph of life over death.

The ritual of an additional cup of wine was certainly born of our own time, yet it already had ample precedent in the history of the Seder; the texts and allusions in our ritual to a fifth cup are all derived from original sources, ranging from the ancient prophets of Israel to modern Israel's Declaration of Independence. A curtain is drawn on a new act in the drama of redemption; but the additional cup is set aside. It is yet to be tasted.

To be sure, our approach to the "Plagues of Egypt" represents a break with the traditional Haggadah. There the recitation of the plagues is integral with the celebration of redemption. On the other hand, the earlier Reform Haggadah eliminated the plagues entirely as unworthy of enlightened sensitivities. Our statement represents a fusion of the particular Jewish experience of deliverance with the universal human longing for redemption.

It is not our intention that this Haggadah be read in its entirety at any one sitting. Our aim is to provide wide latitude and scope for choice. There is a basic text which can be followed through from beginning to end, and, along with it, interpretative readings and songs and situations from which the leader of the group may choose, depending upon circumstance and mood. The structure reveals the course of the basic service, and the variant readings and interpretations are distinguishable from the basic text.

Thanks are due to my colleagues of the Liturgy Committee of the Central Conference of American Rabbis, and to many other rabbis as well, who, over the years, contributed so much to this Haggadah that it can truly be said that the seal of many hands is on it. Rabbi Robert I. Kahn was Chairman of the Liturgy Committee for most of the period during which the Haggadah text was being prepared; and his successor as Chairman of the Committee, Rabbi A. Stanley Dreyfus, saw the process through to conclusion. Rabbi Joseph Glaser, our Executive Vice-President, and Rabbi Malcolm H. Stern of the Central Conference staff served as both masters and servants of the process of preparation.

Anthony Hecht, whose own poetry attests to a profound spiritual gift, gave generously of his time to comments on the stylistic questions, and contributed as well to the enhancement of the text itself. To him I express deep gratitude. Rabbi Lawrence A. Hoffman has written a scholarly and felicitous historical introduction, and Rabbi W. Gunther Plaut has provided practical guidance for

the observance of the Seder. The masterful ability of our illustrator and designer, Leonard Baskin, makes of our new Haggadah a great work of art.

My wife, Tamar, helped Rabbi Malcolm Stern assemble the fine compendium of Passover music and, in succession, Hinda Miller, Dvora Lederman, Cami Maas, and Chaya Friedman diligently prepared the various typescripts of our emerging text. Daniel Dorfman competently and devotedly proofread our text. The Hebrew text was compiled by Aaron Braveman.

I am grateful to Michael Loeb and Carol Weiland for all their help.

My thoughts go back to my teachers at the Hebrew Union College–Jewish Institute of Religion, Professors Samuel S. Cohon, editor of the 1923 Union Haggadah, Alexander Guttman, Eugene Mihaly, and Eric Werner, who first opened my eyes to the spectacular architecture of our liturgy.

Earlier still, as a child, I had already glimpsed the awesome and wonderful kingdom of the sacred into which the Haggadah was an enchanted portal. And so this labor of a round Sabbath of years to which I have endeavored to bring the attitude of מִצְוָה לשם שמים, *mitzvah l'Shem Shamayim*, a free-will offering to the Highest, I dedicate to the memory of my father, Morris Bronstein, ז״ל, the first, on the sacred eve of Passover, to make me aware that I was part of a great processional still being led by a pillar of cloud by day and a pillar of fire by night, from degradation to glory.

ערב שבת „לך לך״ תשל״ד
Erev shabbat lech-lecha, 5734

Rabbi Herbert Bronstein
Glencoe, Illinois

HISTORICAL INTRODUCTION

If one should desire to compress time and space so as to distill and preserve the accumulated Jewish experience of centuries and relive it yearly, he would do well to turn to the Haggadah. The Exodus from Egypt, the seminal event in Jewish history, is related here; and here, too, lie the successive commentaries of the ages on that formative event. For Jews at every time and in every place, seeing themselves in the Haggadah's story, have added their own unique contribution to the annual recounting of the miracle of old.

The original Haggadah was conceived during the tumultuous events of the first century of the common era. It was the product of a Jewish generation wrenched from its roots and splintered within its ranks. Hitherto, the nature of Judaism had been clear. It was a sacrificial system, whose religious festivities revolved about a series of cultic acts performed by a priestly class within the precincts of the Jerusalem Temple. Pilgrims to Jerusalem spent Passover eve consuming the paschal lamb which they had sacrificed in the Temple that afternoon and recounting the tale of the Exodus in what must have been a night of celebration unstructured by any elaborate order of prayer.

But two events of that first century conspired to alter this age-old pattern. One brought about an irrevocable dislocation with the past, while the other shattered the solidarity of the present. The first was the destruction of the Temple in the year 70; the second was the splintering of the Jewish community into disparate sects, nascent Christianity among them. With the past irretrievably severed and rival factions competing for the right to determine the present, the need for a definitive interpretation of Judaism was felt. This the Haggadah was to offer. From now on, Jews would convene annually to recall their past, explain their present, and envision their future.

A format for the annual event was adapted from the surrounding culture. There existed a Hellenistic custom of holding sumptuous banquets accompanied by a philosophic conversation. Such feasts were familiar features of Greco-Roman society, and were easily adaptable for the Seder. The usual food and practices—such as reclining at the table—were imbued with Jewish symbolic value, and the philosophical discourse was transformed into the Haggadah.

The Mishnah, a work compiled at the turn of the third century, describes a Seder much like ours. The *Kiddush* (announcing the sanctity of the day) inaugurated the festivity. Children were urged to ask questions about the uniqueness of the meal. Their queries were answered with a description of the Exodus and a commentary relating that description to the present. The symbolism of the Seder was explained; *Hallel* psalms (Psalms 113–118), sung originally by the

Levites at the Temple, were chanted; and a few final prayers brought the Seder to a close.

The Four Questions, far from being a fixed text for the child to recite, were simply sample queries which his father directed at him if his own natural inquisitiveness failed him. That is, if the child asked nothing at all, his father asked him, in effect, "Didn't you notice that we eat only *matzah* tonight?"

But the Four Questions in our Haggadah come at the beginning of the evening's events. How, we might wonder, could children be expected to notice the oddities of a meal that had yet to be served? The answer, it appears, is that originally the dinner including the symbolic Passover foods was consumed first. Only then did the child comment on what he had seen. The bulk of the Haggadah followed as an explanation of what had already transpired during dinner.

This explanation was in the form of a *midrash*, that is, a running interpretation of the pertinent Biblical narrative, as understood by rabbinic oral tradition. It was constructed to satisfy a basic principle: the Haggadah was to begin with a picture of degradation and to conclude with a portrayal of glory. The Jew at the Seder was to experience the depths of depression in which his ancestors had agonized, and to travel vicariously with them along the historical road leading to the heights of dignity. So the *midrash* began with Jacob's descent into Egypt and the enslavement of his descendents, and concluded with God's entry into history to save His people.

The original Haggadah turned next to an interpretation of the Passover symbols, a remarkable practice, since nowhere else is the Jew obliged to proclaim the rationale behind a commandment. Yet here, Rabban Gamaliel II, the leading sage in the period following the destruction of the Temple, decreed that failure to elucidate the significance of the symbols nullifies the virtue of using them. Again, the Haggadah reflects realistic Jewish concerns arising out of the turmoil of the first century. Jews were not alone in their regard for the Seder. Many Christians believed that Jesus's last supper was a Seder. These Christians—many had once been Jews—probably continued to hold an annual Seder just as they had before their fealty to Jesus of Nazareth. But for them, the Seder rituals carried novel significance. The *matzah*, for example, was the body of their Lord, just as he himself had declared before he died. Now Gamaliel, as the leading Jewish statesman of his time, was undoubtedly aware of this alternative meaning applied to the Passover symbols, so he ordained that Jews everywhere were to state their original Jewish significance. Perhaps this was the reason for transferring dinner to the end of the evening. In its new location, the meal followed the explanation of the symbols. No one was to eat this ritually significant food without first attesting to the proper interpretation of its symbolism.

Opening with the *Kiddush* and questions, then, and moving through the narrative from degradation to glory, the Seder service continued with the interpretation of the symbols and the *Hallel*. Midway in the *Hallel* the meal was served, and the Haggadah was completed thereafter.

But the Haggadah, even at this comparatively early date, transcended mere

recollection of the past. As Jews participated in a meal marking their ancestors' deliverance from Egypt, they could not help but feel all the more deeply their own bondage in Palestine. The destruction of the Temple was but the most dramatic of many hostile events typical of the deteriorating relationship that existed between the Roman regime and its Jewish subjects. Armed conflict continued, reaching yet another climax in an abortive revolt led by a Messianic pretender named Bar Kochba. Legend had it that just as deliverance had occurred on this night so long ago, so ultimate freedom would again come about on Passover. Was it too much to expect that tonight was that night?

So the Haggadah became the story of more than one period of persecution and salvation, as past and present merged in Jewish imagination. The Pharaoh of history personified later oppressors, and the archetypal salvation from the Egyptians carried echoes of Israel's every deliverance through the centuries.

This telescoping of history into one night's celebration can be seen most vividly in the interpretation given to the four cups of wine. They became associated with separate acts of redemption, each indicative of a specific epoch of Jewish history, and each presumably called for by a specific Biblical promise. One rabbi in fact, Rabbi Tarfon, used to drink a *fifth* cup at his Seder. He traced it to yet a fifth Biblical prophecy, one that differed from the other four in that it had yet to be fulfilled. For Rabbi Tarfon, the Seder was more than just a lesson in history. It was the making of history, the night of ultimate salvation, God's reentry into history to save Israel again, as He had done so long ago.

Although traditional Haggadahs eventually dispensed with this fifth cup, the custom of anticipating final redemption on Passover eve was never entirely lost. A fifth cup remained on the table during the meal and became known as the cup of Elijah, the prophet expected to herald this ultimate deliverance. So, today, at the meal's end, after participating in the story of the Exodus and journeying with Israel of old from degradation to glory, the Jew reaches out in spirit for that ultimate glory, promised through the prophets and described by the rabbis: the Messianic age, the end of subjugation for all, capsulated in the words "Next year in Jerusalem!"

Later generations inherited the Haggadah of the Mishnah. Though they did not alter its essential nature, they did expand its contents. The Talmud, for example, provided alternative interpretations of the concept of degradation. One rabbi, Samuel, understood it to mean physical servitude under Pharaoh. His colleague, Rav, took it to denote slavery of the spirit, inherent in early Israel's idolatry. The Haggadah adopted both views in the form of thematic introductions to the *midrash*.

The traditional Haggadah today is the legacy of our Ashkenazic forebears. Like Israelites in Egypt and Jews in first-century Palestine, Rhineland Jewry, too, suffered: in their case, from marauding bands of Crusaders. These same generations that were moved to remember their dead through the innovations of *yizkor* and *yahrzeit* must have met on Passover eve dreaming of deliverance and even revenge. They expressed these emotions by imploring God to pour out

vengeance on their persecutors. It was Ashkenazic Jewry, also, that adopted the many songs that we sing at our Seder. Some songs, like "Dayenu," had been optional elements in previous Haggadahs, but were now incorporated as integral parts of the service. Other songs were newly appended to the service and remain with us today. The familiar "Had Gadya," for example, based on a secular folk song, was introduced as a parable of Israel's history. "Adir Hu" also was a popular song at first. In fact, it was probably composed in the vernacular and sung on all holidays before it was translated into Hebrew and reserved for the Haggadah. And even after newly written prayers ceased being introduced into the Haggadah text, Jews everywhere saw themselves as if they personally had been delivered from Egypt. Conversely, as if impervious to the artificial limitations imposed by the logic of time, they brought the Exodus of history up to date by writing marginal commentaries which extracted veiled allusions to the present from the Haggadah's description of the past.

The Haggadah offered here can be seen as a continuation of its predecessors. It contains the Haggadah's essence and attempts to relate the past to both the conditions of the present and our hopes for the future. The Talmud's alternative interpretations of the degradation (pp. 34–37) still introduce the story of Passover, but their philosophical distinction is made manifest. The midrashic answer, which spoke so well to first-century Jews, has been replaced with a modern equivalent, which, like its forerunner, combines the Biblical narrative with relevant commentary. The *Hallel* (p. 71) and the grace after meals (p. 61) remain, but the prayer for revenge instituted during Crusader times has been replaced with an alternate ritual which evokes fundamental moments of Jewish history and existence (pp. 68–71). The fifth cup, so long absent, has been restored as a symbol of our faith in the future (p. 77). Throughout, old songs have been retained, and new material has been added in the form of optional readings on the Haggadah text. Even the use of English has good traditional justification. Some of the most illustrious rabbis in our history—Rashi included—translated their Haggadahs, either in part or entirely, into the vernacular, so insistent were they that its message be understood by all present. The Shulḥan Aruḥ, in fact, prescribes the recitation of the Four Questions in the vernacular, and notes without objection the custom of reciting the whole Haggadah in a language all may comprehend.

The Haggadah mirrors the Jews who composed it. It is not so much recited as experienced. It is hoped that this Haggadah may prove to be an authentic extension of its predecessors, providing an image of our past, a portrait of our present, and a testimony to our faith in the future.

Lawrence A. Hoffman

PREPARING FOR THE SEDER

The Seder is our festive introduction to a full week of sacred observance celebrating a number of events and ideas: the birth of the Jewish people, its struggle for freedom, God's role in the history of the people of Israel, and its role in God's purposes. The Seder is a unique opportunity for religious sharing with family, friends, and guests; for enhancing the meaning of Judaism and rejoicing in its beauty; and for a personal experience of the mysterious unfolding of our people's story, the wonder of our redemption, past, present, and future.

The household. The home is the center of the Jewish way of life. The household must be prepared for this week of fuller Jewish observance. Whether or not the Seder itself takes place in your home, the household should reflect the special nature of the Passover week.

During *Pesaḥ*, food and its preparation are important. The following recommendations are presented in the hope that our families will choose to intensify their observance and thus their awareness of Passover's meaning.

In the manner of "spring cleaning," thoroughly prepare your home for Passover. This, along with the different foods, dishes, and utensils that should be set aside and used only during Passover, will recall the special sanctity of the time, and impress themselves especially upon the imagination of our children, heightening the fascination of the festival.

Removing ḥametz. *Ḥametz* is that food which has been or could become subject to a leavening process, or food that has come in contact with leavened foods. *Matzah* is a bread baked without leavening. Prime examples of *ḥametz* are ordinary bread and crackers and cakes; breakfast cereals and pies made from leavened flour; and whisky. The common means of Passover baking are *matzah* meal (made from ground *matzah*) and potato flour. It is suggested that the family make a common decision as to what practice they will adhere to in their home. The *ḥametz* can be stored in an out-of-the way place during the week.

The searching for leaven (B'dikat Ḥametz). If the *ḥametz* has been removed, then one cannot eat bread the day before the Seder meal. The natural temptation is to replace the bread with *matzah*. However, to heighten the anticipation and the meaning of eating *matzah* at the Seder itself, no *matzah* is eaten at least a full day before the Seder (some say two weeks prior). Breakfast and lunch on the day of the Seder then would include neither bread nor breadstuffs nor *matzah*, but Passover foods other than *matzah* can be eaten.

The ceremony of *B'dikat Ḥametz*, the searching for leaven, signifies that the

home has been made into a Passover sanctuary. By the morning of the Seder, the house must be ready for the Passover week and *ḥametz* removed from use. Thus, for the rite of "searching for the *ḥametz*" (a dramatic and even compelling experience, particularly for children) takes place on the night before the first Seder night. At various places in the home, a parent hides pieces of bread wrapped in paper. In the dark, the children, with flashlights or other illumination, search them out. They are gathered in a bag or paper container and are disposed of. Some follow the literal practice of burning *ḥametz* in the fireplace or outside. The disposal of the *ḥametz* is accompanied with this brief prayer:

בָּרוּךְ אַתָּה יְיָ אֱלֹהֵינוּ מֶלֶךְ הָעוֹלָם אֲשֶׁר קִדְּשָׁנוּ בְּמִצְוֹתָיו וְצִוָּנוּ עַל בִּיעוּר חָמֵץ.

As we prepare for Passover, and observe the rite of the removal of ḥametz, *leaven, we praise You, O God, who hallows our lives with commandments.*

Preparing for the Seder. The Seder is vastly more than a family dinner observed in a casual or haphazard manner, but is rather a religious drama of the highest significance. Preparation is needed not only by those who prepare the dinner and conduct the Seder service, but also by others who attend.

Arrange to leave your place of work a little earlier than usual, so that you may properly prepare yourself for the arrival of the holy day. Whoever conducts the Seder sees to it that those who attend are provided with Haggadahs. It is not intended that this Haggadah be used in its entirety at any one Seder. Choose from the Haggadah ahead of time interpretive passages (not part of the basic text) which are suitable for the group and decide which passages to omit. One interpretation may be used one year and another the next. Go over the prayers and readings that you expect to read or sing yourself, and mark those parts that you will assign to others. If possible, let others know of their parts in advance. The children too are given parts in advance, so that they may have ample time to prepare. In planning for the singing, you may wish to use recordings prepared for this Haggadah by the Central Conference of American Rabbis. Others in the attending group may be able to help you with the musical preparations. Encourage informal participation, questioning, and spirited discussion.

Plan the overall content and timing of the Seder. It consists of three parts: the service before dinner, dinner, readings and songs afterward. To achieve the fullest religious content, as well as pure enjoyment, scale the duration to the makeup of the group. Each family is different; each leader of a Seder lends his own personality to the observance. The aim is a celebration, serious yet relaxed, and filled with gaiety and drama. By the manner in which you conduct the Seder, invite into your home the presence of the Divine. The joy of a Jew celebrating, in the midst of freedom, the birth of his people, and the greatness of God—what greater ingredients can there be! Make full use of them.

The table setting. Set the table in a most festive manner. Candles should be provided for the Seder. In front of the leader place a special Seder plate. On this plate arrange the following:

Three separate pieces of matzah. Three whole pieces of *matzah* should be placed in either a special cloth *matzah* cover with three sections or in a napkin folded over twice. These three *matzot* represent the two traditional loaves set out in the ancient Temple during the festival day and the extra *matzah* symbolic of Passover.

A roasted shankbone, burned or scorched, representing the ancient Passover sacrifice.

Parsley or any green herbs, the growth of springtime, the green of hope and renewal.

The top part of the horseradish root (*maror*), symbolic of the bitterness that our forefathers experienced in Egypt, and in a contemporary sense, the lot of all who are enslaved.

Ḥaroset, representing the mortar which our ancestors used in doing Pharaoh's labor. One recipe for *ḥaroset* follows:

> Combine apples (at least a half apple per person), peeled and chopped fine or grated, with chopped walnuts or pecans, to which chopped or mashed raisins, dates, prunes, or apricots may be added. Add cinnamon and wine to taste.

It is a lovely tradition for members of the family to join prior to the Seder in preparing the various items for the Seder plate.

A roasted egg, representing the *ḥagigah* or festival offering, a symbol of life itself, a triumph of life over death.

The cup for Elijah. A special and fine cup filled with wine is placed prominently on the table. In parable, the Prophet Elijah (herald of redemption) at some time during the Seder visits every Jewish home and tastes the cup set aside for him. It is a dramatic moment when a child, or children, open the door for Elijah, and a sense of mystery is always associated with this moment of the Seder.

Symbolic foods for the participants. Either in a setting for each person or in serving plates around the table, there should be a wine glass, *ḥaroset*, prepared horseradish, salt water (many put half a hardboiled egg in the dish of salt water) for dipping the parsley or green herbs, and *matzah*.

The empty chair. It is customary to leave an extra chair at the table denoting those of our people who live in lands where they cannot celebrate the Passover as free men. They are remembered in the Jewish household on this night.

The dinner. Many cookbooks are available that provide a multitude of culinary suggestions for the preparation of the Seder. One ritual item, Passover wine, is constant.

Hiding the afikoman. The *afikoman* is the half *matzah* that is set aside during the breaking of the *matzah* early in the Seder (see p. 26). An old tradition held that

the group could not leave the Seder table unless all had tasted of the *afikoman*. In connection with this, and in order to arouse and maintain the interest of the children and to provide some entertainment for them, a practice developed of hiding and searching for the *afikoman*. Some time during the meal the leader hides the *afikoman* wrapped in a napkin, trying to elude the watchful observance of the children, whose endeavor it is to search out its hiding place. Prizes might be awarded to all who participated, with a special gift to the one who actually found it.

Customs of Passover. Through the altered "life-style" of Passover week, we retain our consciousness of its meaning; we bear witness to its message for our fellow Jews and our non-Jewish associates.

Food during the Passover week. Minimal observance would consist of not eating bread either at home or elsewhere. More religious observance would consist of not eating any *ḥametz*. For lunch, it may be convenient to bring food to work or school.

Synagogue attendance. The Bible prescribes that no work is done on the first and seventh days of Passover. A lovely Seder, family worship the following morning, and a festival day together add immeasurably to Passover observance.

The Yizkor. Memorial prayers are recited in the synagogue on the last morning of Passover. An affirmation of the triumph of the spirit over death is a hallmark of our major holidays. By all means, take your children to the *Yizkor* service, which enlarges our love as well as our vision.

The conclusion of Passover. If the last day of Passover happens to fall on the Sabbath, the day is ended with the ceremony of *Havdalah* (*Shabbat Manual*, pp. 34 ff.).

Ḥag Sameaḥ. As is the custom in greeting one another during Passover, so we now say חג שמח, *Ḥag Sameaḥ*, or, as in older parlance, a Good Yom Tov!

W. Gunther Plaut

A NOTE

This is a joyful but serious religious service. Its locus is the miraculous deliverance of the Children of Israel from Egyptian bondage, through peril and in the face of impossible odds, to the gifts of divine sustenance in the wilderness (the quails and *manna*) and of divine wisdom (the Law) at Mount Sinai—a sustenance, therefore, of the body and the soul—and at last into the freedom and beatitude of the Holy Land. This pilgrimage represents the spiritual journey from darkness into light that we all must try to make in the course of our lives. Its shape is that of a dramatic and miraculous narrative; and for both educative and spiritual reasons (which are never far apart) it seems important that the excitement and wonder of the story itself, the events that happened on that night which make it different from all other nights—and not only the events of that night, but of the entire deliverance—should not be lost sight of. The rejoicing that ends the service is plausible only if all the preceding events are fully realized—not just the pain and humiliation of bondage, but the difficulties and excitement of the deliverance. So the service ends not only in joy but in clarification: a movement from darkness to light—we understand what we had not known, or had forgotten, or had neglected, or had misunderstood before.

Anthony Hecht

עץ
חיים היא
למחזיקים
בה

הַגָּדָה שֶׁל פֶּסַח

A PASSOVER HAGGADAH

קַדֵּשׁ

𝄞 1

KADESH, SANCTIFICATION OF THE DAY

Leader

Now in the presence of loved ones and friends,
before us the emblems of festive rejoicing,
we gather for our sacred celebration.
With the household of Israel, our elders and young ones,
linking and bonding the past with the future,
we heed once again the divine call
to service.
Living our story that is told for all peoples,
whose shining conclusion is yet to unfold,
we gather to observe the Passover,
as it is written:

וּשְׁמַרְתֶּם אֶת־הַמַּצּוֹת כִּי בְּעֶצֶם הַיּוֹם הַזֶּה הוֹצֵאתִי אֶת־צִבְאוֹתֵיכֶם מֵאֶרֶץ
מִצְרָיִם וּשְׁמַרְתֶּם אֶת־הַיּוֹם הַזֶּה לְדֹרֹתֵיכֶם חֻקַּת עוֹלָם׃

Group

Exodus 12:17

You shall keep the Feast of Unleavened Bread, for on this very day I brought your hosts out of Egypt. You shall observe this day throughout the generations as a practice for all times.

Leader

We assemble in fulfillment of the *mitzvah:*

זָכוֹר אֶת־הַיּוֹם הַזֶּה אֲשֶׁר יְצָאתֶם מִמִּצְרַיִם מִבֵּית עֲבָדִים כִּי בְּחֹזֶק יָד הוֹצִיא
יְהוָֹה אֶתְכֶם מִזֶּה׃

Group

Exodus 13:3

Remember the day on which you went forth from Egypt, from the house of bondage, and how God freed you with a mighty hand.

𝄞 1. Music and lyrics for the songs begin on page 97.

הַדְלָקַת הַנֵּרוֹת

Lighting the Festival Candles

(One of these meditations may be used.)

Happy are those of steadfast faith
Who still can bless the light of candles
Shining in the darkness. . . .
Rejoice, O Earth, in those who keep the way,
For there is still song for them within you.

May the festival lights we now kindle
Inspire us to use our powers
To heal and not to harm,
To help and not to hinder,
To bless and not to curse,
To serve You, O God of freedom.

* * *

(The candles are lighted as the blessing is recited or chanted.)

בָּרוּךְ אַתָּה יְיָ אֱלֹהֵינוּ מֶלֶךְ הָעוֹלָם אֲשֶׁר קִדְּשָׁנוּ בְּמִצְוֹתָיו וְצִוָּנוּ 𝄞 2,3
לְהַדְלִיק נֵר שֶׁל (שַׁבָּת וְשֶׁל) יוֹם טוֹב.

Baruḥ Atah Adonai Eloheinu Meleḥ ha-olam asher kidshanu b'mitzvo-tav v'tzivanu l'hadlik neir shel (*shabbat v'shel*) *yom tov.*

In praising God we say that all life is sacred.
In kindling festive lights,
we preserve life's sanctity.
With every holy light we kindle,
the world is brightened to a higher harmony.
We praise Thee, God, majestic sovereign of all life,
Who hallows our lives with commandments
and bids us kindle festive holy light.

כּוֹס קִדּוּשׁ

Kos Kiddush, The First Cup—the Cup of Sanctification

Leader

Our story tells that in diverse ways, with different words, God gave promises of freedom to our people. With cups of wine we recall each one of them, as now, the first:

Group

אֲנִי יְהֹוָה וְהוֹצֵאתִי אֶתְכֶם מִתַּחַת סִבְלֹת מִצְרָיִם:

I am יהוה and *I will free you* from the burdens of the Egyptians. ***Exodus 6:6***

כחליית ההרים
דרדר כחול
אירוס הלבנון

Leader

We take up the Kiddush cup and proclaim the holiness of this Day of Deliverance!

(Begin here on the Sabbath.)

וַיְהִי־עֶרֶב וַיְהִי־בֹקֶר יוֹם הַשִּׁשִּׁי:
וַיְכֻלּוּ הַשָּׁמַיִם וְהָאָרֶץ וְכָל־צְבָאָם: וַיְכַל אֱלֹהִים בַּיּוֹם הַשְּׁבִיעִי מְלַאכְתּוֹ אֲשֶׁר 𝄞 4
עָשָׂה וַיִּשְׁבֹּת בַּיּוֹם הַשְּׁבִיעִי מִכָּל־מְלַאכְתּוֹ אֲשֶׁר עָשָׂה: וַיְבָרֶךְ אֱלֹהִים אֶת־יוֹם
הַשְּׁבִיעִי וַיְקַדֵּשׁ אֹתוֹ כִּי בוֹ שָׁבַת מִכָּל־מְלַאכְתּוֹ אֲשֶׁר־בָּרָא אֱלֹהִים לַעֲשׂוֹת:

It was evening and morning, a sixth day, when the heaven and the earth were finished and all their array. And on the seventh day God finished all the work of creation. And God made cessation on the seventh day from all the work which God had done. And God blessed the seventh day and made it holy, for upon it, God made cessation from all the work of creating. *Genesis 2:1–3*

(On weekdays begin here.)

בָּרוּךְ אַתָּה יְיָ אֱלֹהֵינוּ מֶלֶךְ הָעוֹלָם בּוֹרֵא פְּרִי הַגָּפֶן: 𝄞 5

Baruḥ Atah Adonai Eloheinu Meleḥ ha-olam borei p'ri ha-gafen.

We praise Thee, O God, Sovereign of Existence, Who creates the fruit of the vine!

בָּרוּךְ אַתָּה יְיָ אֱלֹהֵינוּ מֶלֶךְ הָעוֹלָם אֲשֶׁר בָּחַר־בָּנוּ מִכָּל־עָם וְרוֹמְמָנוּ מִכָּל־לָשׁוֹן וְקִדְּשָׁנוּ בְּמִצְוֹתָיו. וַתִּתֶּן־לָנוּ יְיָ אֱלֹהֵינוּ בְּאַהֲבָה (שַׁבָּתוֹת לִמְנוּחָה וּ) מוֹעֲדִים לְשִׂמְחָה חַגִּים וּזְמַנִּים לְשָׂשׂוֹן אֶת־יוֹם (הַשַּׁבָּת הַזֶּה וְאֶת־יוֹם) חַג הַמַּצּוֹת הַזֶּה זְמַן חֵרוּתֵנוּ (בְּאַהֲבָה) מִקְרָא קֹדֶשׁ זֵכֶר לִיצִיאַת מִצְרָיִם. כִּי בָנוּ בָחַרְתָּ וְאוֹתָנוּ קִדַּשְׁתָּ מִכָּל־הָעַמִּים (וְשַׁבָּת) וּמוֹעֲדֵי קָדְשֶׁךָ (בְּאַהֲבָה וּבְרָצוֹן) בְּשִׂמְחָה וּבְשָׂשׂוֹן הִנְחַלְתָּנוּ. בָּרוּךְ אַתָּה יְיָ מְקַדֵּשׁ (הַשַּׁבָּת וְ) יִשְׂרָאֵל וְהַזְּמַנִּים:

We praise Thee, God, Sovereign of Existence! You have called us for service from among the peoples, and have hallowed our lives with commandments. In love Thou hast given us [Sabbaths for rest,] festivals for rejoicing, seasons of celebration, this Festival of *Matzot*, the time of our freedom, a commemoration of the Exodus from Egypt. Praised are You, יהוה our God, Who gave us this joyful heritage and Who sanctifies [the Sabbath,] Israel, and the festivals.

(When the Seder is held on Saturday night, the following Havdalah is added.)

בָּרוּךְ אַתָּה יְיָ אֱלֹהֵינוּ מֶלֶךְ הָעוֹלָם בּוֹרֵא מְאוֹרֵי הָאֵשׁ.

Baruḥ Atah Adonai Eloheinu Meleḥ ha-olam borei m'orei ha-eish.

בָּרוּךְ אַתָּה יְיָ אֱלֹהֵינוּ מֶלֶךְ הָעוֹלָם הַמַּבְדִּיל בֵּין קֹדֶשׁ לְחֹל בֵּין אוֹר לְחֹשֶׁךְ בֵּין יִשְׂרָאֵל לָעַמִּים, בֵּין יוֹם הַשְּׁבִיעִי לְשֵׁשֶׁת יְמֵי הַמַּעֲשֶׂה. בֵּין קְדֻשַּׁת שַׁבָּת לִקְדֻשַּׁת יוֹם טוֹב הִבְדַּלְתָּ, וְאֶת יוֹם הַשְּׁבִיעִי מִשֵּׁשֶׁת יְמֵי הַמַּעֲשֶׂה קִדַּשְׁתָּ; הִבְדַּלְתָּ וְקִדַּשְׁתָּ אֶת עַמְּךָ יִשְׂרָאֵל בִּקְדֻשָּׁתֶךָ. בָּרוּךְ אַתָּה יְיָ הַמַּבְדִּיל בֵּין קֹדֶשׁ לְקֹדֶשׁ.

We praise Thee, our God, Sovereign of Existence, Who creates the lights of fire, Who teaches us to know light from darkness, sacred from profane. As we sense the holy, and sanctify the Sabbath among the days of the week, we are ourselves consecrated. We learn to endow each sacred day with its own holiness. We praise Thee, our God, Who has given us to know the holy.

(On Sabbaths and weekdays continue here.)

בָּרוּךְ אַתָּה יְיָ אֱלֹהֵינוּ מֶלֶךְ הָעוֹלָם שֶׁהֶחֱיָנוּ וְקִיְּמָנוּ וְהִגִּיעָנוּ לַזְּמַן הַזֶּה:

Baruḥ Atah Adonai Eloheinu Meleḥ ha-olam sheh-heh-ḥeh-yanu v'ki-y'manu v'higi-anu lazman hazeh.

We praise Thee, O Lord our God, Sovereign of Existence, Who has kept us in life, sustained us, and brought us to this festive season.

(All drink the first cup of wine.)

כַּרְפַּס

KARPAS, REBIRTH AND RENEWAL

(In the spring of the year, the season of rebirth and renewal, on the festival of Pesaḥ, *we read from the Song of Songs. The poetry of nature and of love evokes, as well, the love between God and the people Israel, and their Covenant-betrothal.)*

Leader

𝄞 6

Song of Songs 2:10–12

Arise my beloved, my fair one,
And come away;
For lo, the winter is past.
Flowers appear on the earth,
The time of singing is here.
The song of the dove
Is heard in our land.

עָנָה דוֹדִי וְאָמַר לִי
קוּמִי לָךְ רַעְיָתִי יָפָתִי וּלְכִי־לָךְ:
כִּי־הִנֵּה הַסְּתָו עָבָר הַגֶּשֶׁם חָלַף הָלַךְ לוֹ:
הַנִּצָּנִים נִרְאוּ בָאָרֶץ עֵת הַזָּמִיר הִגִּיעַ
וְקוֹל הַתּוֹר נִשְׁמַע בְּאַרְצֵנוּ:

7:13

Let us go down to the vineyards
To see if the vines have budded.
There will I give you my love.

נַשְׁכִּימָה לַכְּרָמִים
נִרְאֶה אִם־פָּרְחָה הַגֶּפֶן
פִּתַּח הַסְּמָדַר הֵנֵצוּ הָרִמּוֹנִים
שָׁם אֶתֵּן אֶת־דֹּדַי לָךְ:

(Each person takes some greens and dips them in salt water.)

Group

בָּרוּךְ אַתָּה יְיָ אֱלֹהֵינוּ מֶלֶךְ הָעוֹלָם בּוֹרֵא פְּרִי הָאֲדָמָה:

Baruḥ Atah Adonai Eloheinu Meleḥ ha-olam borei p'ri ha-adamah.
Praised are You, *Adonai*, Sovereign of Existence,
Who creates the fruit of the earth.

(Eat the greens.)

יַחַץ

YAḤATZ, A BOND FORMED BY SHARING

Leader

Now I break the middle *matzah* and conceal one half as the *afikoman*. Later we will share it, as in days of old the Passover offering itself was shared at this service in Jerusalem. Among people everywhere, sharing of bread forms a bond of fellowship. For the sake of our redemption, we say together the ancient words which join us with our own people and with all who are in need, with the wrongly imprisoned and the beggar in the street. For our redemption is bound up with the deliverance from bondage of people everywhere.

Group

הָא לַחְמָא עַנְיָא דִּי אֲכָלוּ אֲבָהָתָנָא בְּאַרְעָא דְמִצְרָיִם. כָּל־דִּכְפִין יֵיתֵי וְיֵכֻל. 𝄞 7
כָּל־דִּצְרִיךְ יֵיתֵי וְיִפְסַח. הָשַׁתָּא הָכָא. לְשָׁנָה הַבָּאָה בְּאַרְעָא דְיִשְׂרָאֵל. הָשַׁתָּא
עַבְדֵי. לְשָׁנָה הַבָּאָה בְּנֵי חוֹרִין:

This is the bread of affliction,
the poor bread,
which our ancestors ate in the land of Egypt.
Let all who are hungry come and eat.
Let all who are in want
share the hope of Passover.
As we celebrate here,
we join with our people everywhere.
This year we celebrate here.
Next year in the land of Israel.
Now we are all still in bonds.
Next year may all be free.

Let all who are in want
share the hope of Passover.

הא
לחמא עניא די אכלו
אבהתנא בארעא דמצרים
כל דכפין ייתי ויכול. כל דצריך
ייתי ויפסח. השתא הכא לשנה
הבאה בארעא דישראל. השתא
עבדי. לשנה הבאה בני חורין:

מוֹצִיא מַצָּה מָרוֹר

MOTZI, MATZAH, MAROR

(This section and "Koreḥ," below, may be deferred, if desired, according to the long-standing custom, to page 60, following the second cup of wine and immediately before the meal.)

(The uppermost of the three matzot *is broken and distributed among the group. Then all read together:)*

בָּרוּךְ אַתָּה יְיָ אֱלֹהֵינוּ מֶלֶךְ הָעוֹלָם הַמּוֹצִיא לֶחֶם מִן הָאָרֶץ:

Baruḥ Atah Adonai Eloheinu Meleḥ ha-olam ha-motzi lehem min ha-aretz.
We praise Thee, O God, Sovereign of Existence, Who brings forth bread from the earth.

בָּרוּךְ אַתָּה יְיָ אֱלֹהֵינוּ מֶלֶךְ הָעוֹלָם אֲשֶׁר קִדְּשָׁנוּ בְּמִצְוֹתָיו וְצִוָּנוּ עַל אֲכִילַת מַצָּה:

Baruḥ Atah Adonai Eloheinu Meleḥ ha-olam asher kidshanu b'mitzvo-tav v'tzivanu al aḥilat matzah.
We praise Thee, O God, Sovereign of Existence, Who hallows our lives with commandments, Who has commanded us regarding the eating of *matzah*. *(Eat the* matzah.*)*

(A bit of horseradish is placed on a piece of matzah *and the following blessing is said.)*

בָּרוּךְ אַתָּה יְיָ אֱלֹהֵינוּ מֶלֶךְ הָעוֹלָם אֲשֶׁר קִדְּשָׁנוּ בְּמִצְוֹתָיו וְצִוָּנוּ עַל אֲכִילַת מָרוֹר:

Baruḥ Atah Adonai Eloheinu Meleḥ ha-olam asher kidshanu b'mitzvo-tav v'tzivanu al aḥilat maror.
We praise Thee, O God, Sovereign of Existence, Who hallows our lives through commandments, Who has commanded us regarding the eating of *maror*. *(Eat the* maror.*)*

כּוֹרֵךְ

KOREḤ, CONTINUITY WITH PAST TRADITION

Leader

זֵכֶר לְמִקְדָּשׁ כְּהִלֵּל: כֵּן עָשָׂה הִלֵּל בִּזְמַן שֶׁבֵּית הַמִּקְדָּשׁ הָיָה קַיָּם. הָיָה כּוֹרֵךְ פֶּסַח מַצָּה וּמָרוֹר וְאוֹכֵל בְּיַחַד. לְקַיֵּם מַה שֶּׁנֶּאֱמַר: עַל־מַצּוֹת וּמְרֹרִים יֹאכְלֻהוּ:

Preserving a bond with the observance of our ancestors, we follow a practice of Hillel, from the time when the Temple stood. He combined the *matzah* and *maror* and ate them together, so that he might observe

the precept handed down to him, exactly as his father before him:
Numbers 9:11 "They shall eat the *paschal lamb* with *matzah* and *maror together.*"

Group

Together they shall be: the *matzah* of freedom, the *maror* of slavery.
For in the time of freedom, there is knowledge of servitude.
And in the time of bondage, the hope of redemption.

(*According to an ancient custom,* maror *and* haroset *are eaten between two pieces of* matzah.)

Four Questions

Leader

בִּנְעָרֵינוּ וּבִזְקֵנֵינוּ נֵלֵךְ בְּבָנֵינוּ וּבִבְנוֹתֵנוּ בְּצֹאנֵנוּ וּבִבְקָרֵנוּ נֵלֵךְ כִּי חַג־יְהוָֹה לָנוּ׃

Exodus 10:9 "We will go, young and old. We will go with our sons and our daughters . . . for we must observe unto God a festival."
So it was said before the first Passover observance.
To this day, our children continue to join in our observance.

A Child or Children

𝄞 8,9 מַה נִּשְׁתַּנָּה הַלַּיְלָה הַזֶּה מִכָּל הַלֵּילוֹת.
שֶׁבְּכָל הַלֵּילוֹת אָנוּ אוֹכְלִין חָמֵץ וּמַצָּה, הַלַּיְלָה הַזֶּה כֻּלּוֹ מַצָּה.
שֶׁבְּכָל הַלֵּילוֹת אָנוּ אוֹכְלִין שְׁאָר יְרָקוֹת, הַלַּיְלָה הַזֶּה מָרוֹר.
שֶׁבְּכָל הַלֵּילוֹת אֵין אָנוּ מַטְבִּילִין אֲפִילוּ פַּעַם אֶחָת, הַלַּיְלָה הַזֶּה שְׁתֵּי פְעָמִים.
שֶׁבְּכָל הַלֵּילוֹת אָנוּ אוֹכְלִין בֵּין יוֹשְׁבִין וּבֵין מְסֻבִּין, הַלַּיְלָה הַזֶּה כֻּלָּנוּ מְסֻבִּין.

Why is this night different from all the other nights?
On all other nights, we eat either leavened bread or *matzah*; on this night—only *matzah.*
On all other nights, we eat all kinds of herbs; on this night, we especially eat bitter herbs.
On all other nights, we do not dip herbs at all; on this night we dip them twice.
On all other nights, we eat in an ordinary manner; tonight we dine with special ceremony.

אַרְבַּעַת־הַבָּנִים

The Four Children

Leader

בָּרוּךְ הַמָּקוֹם בָּרוּךְ הוּא. בָּרוּךְ שֶׁנָּתַן תּוֹרָה לְעַמּוֹ יִשְׂרָאֵל. בָּרוּךְ הוּא: כְּנֶגֶד אַרְבָּעָה בָנִים דִּבְּרָה תוֹרָה. אֶחָד חָכָם. וְאֶחָד רָשָׁע. וְאֶחָד תָּם. וְאֶחָד שֶׁאֵינוֹ יוֹדֵעַ לִשְׁאוֹל:

Four times the Torah bids us tell our children of the Exodus from Egypt. Four times the Torah repeats: "And you shall tell your child on that day. . . ." From this, our tradition infers that there are different kinds of people. To each we respond in a different manner, according to the question, the situation, and the need.

A Participant

חָכָם מָה הוּא אוֹמֵר, מָה הָעֵדֹת וְהַחֻקִּים וְהַמִּשְׁפָּטִים אֲשֶׁר צִוָּה יְיָ אֱלֹהֵינוּ אֶתְכֶם:
וְאַף אַתָּה אֱמָר־לוֹ כְּהִלְכוֹת הַפֶּסַח אֵין מַפְטִירִין אַחַר הַפֶּסַח אֲפִיקוֹמָן:

The wise person asks, "What are the precepts, laws, and observances *Deuteronomy 6:20*
which יהוה our God commanded us?" In response we should explain the observances of the Passover thoroughly, the very last one of which is: After the Passover Seder, we do not turn to other kinds of entertainment.

Group

It is the wise who want to know the service it is theirs to do.

A Participant

רָשָׁע מָה הוּא אוֹמֵר. מָה הָעֲבֹדָה הַזֹּאת לָכֶם. לָכֶם וְלֹא לוֹ. וּלְפִי שֶׁהוֹצִיא אֶת עַצְמוֹ מִן הַכְּלָל כָּפַר בְּעִקָּר. וְאַף אַתָּה הַקְהֵה אֶת־שִׁנָּיו וֶאֱמוֹר לוֹ. בַּעֲבוּר זֶה עָשָׂה יְיָ לִי בְּצֵאתִי מִמִּצְרָיִם. לִי וְלֹא לָךְ. אִלּוּ הָיִיתָ שָׁם, לֹא הָיִיתָ נִגְאָל:

The wicked person says, "What is this observance to *you*?" Since he says *Exodus 12:26*
"to *you*" and not "to us," he rejects essentials of our faith: the unity of God and the community of Israel. Thus we respond sharply: "It is because of what God did for *me* when *I* went forth from Egypt—'for *me*,' that is, and not 'for *you*' . . . for had you been there, you would not have known redemption."

Group

The wicked one withdraws the self from anything beyond the self; and thus, from the joy of redemption.

You shall tell your child on that day.

A Participant

תָּם מָה הוּא אוֹמֵר. מַה־זֹּאת. וְאָמַרְתָּ אֵלָיו. בְּחֹזֶק יָד הוֹצִיאָנוּ יְיָ מִמִּצְרַיִם
מִבֵּית עֲבָדִים:

When the simple person asks, "What is this?" Then we say, "With a *Exodus 13:14*
mighty arm God freed us from Egypt, from the house of bondage."

Group

To the person of open simplicity, give a straightforward answer; for
"The Torah of God makes wise the simple." *Psalm 19:7*

A Participant

וְשֶׁאֵינוֹ יוֹדֵעַ לִשְׁאוֹל. אַתְּ פְּתַח לוֹ. שֶׁנֶּאֱמַר וְהִגַּדְתָּ לְבִנְךָ בַּיּוֹם הַהוּא לֵאמֹר.
בַּעֲבוּר זֶה עָשָׂה יְיָ לִי בְּצֵאתִי מִמִּצְרָיִם:

With the person unable to ask, you must begin yourself, as it is written:
"You shall tell your child on that day, saying: 'This is because of what *Exodus 13:8*
God did for me when I went free from Egypt.' "

Group

With one who has no need to know, no will to serve, "You must begin yourself" to awaken the need, to give the will.

Leader

As in the pages of our histories, so too in the events of our time, in the encounters of our daily lives, these persons, the wise, the wicked, the simple, the one unable to ask, reappear in various guises. To this day, their questions must be pondered and answers sought, the story given life and meaning.

(*The following readings suggest various interpretations of the Four Children.* *The Seder text continues on page 34.*)

The Four Children

From a Wise Son to Others

The monument . . . shall serve as a reminder for us who have survived to re-

This symbol denotes optional readings.

* * * Three stars mark resumption of main text.

main loyal to our people and to the moral principles cherished by our fathers. Only through such loyalty may we hope to survive this age of moral decay. . . . Let us clearly recognize and never forget this: that mutual cooperation and the furtherance of living ties between the Jews of all lands is our sole physical and moral protection in the present situation. But for the future our hope lies in overcoming the general moral abasement which today gravely menaces the very existence of mankind.

Albert Einstein before the monument to the martyred Jews of the Warsaw Ghetto, April 19, 1948

*

Jews Who Repudiate Themselves—They Say to *You*

The Jew who repudiates himself, claiming to do so for the sake of humanity, will inevitably repudiate humanity in the end. A Jew fulfills his role as a man only from inside his Jewishness. Only by accepting his Jewishness can he attain universality.

Elie Wiesel

*

The Seder of "The Simple"

Then my wife woke me, and it was evening, and she said to me: "Why don't you celebrate the Seder like all other Jews?" Said I: "What do you want with me? I am an ignorant man, and my father was an ignorant man, and I don't know what to do and what not to do. But one thing I know: Our fathers and mothers were in captivity in the land of the Gypsies, and we have a God, and He led them out, and into freedom. And see: now we are again in captivity and I know, and I tell you that God will lead us to freedom too." And then I saw before me a table, and the cloth gleamed like the sun, and on it were platters with *matzot* and eggs and other dishes, and bottles of red wine. I ate of the *matzot* and eggs and drank of the wine, and gave my wife to eat and to drink. And then I was overcome with joy, and lifted my cup to God, and said: "See, God, I drink this cup to You! And do You lean down to us and make us free!"

Ḥasidic story retold by Martin Buber

*

"I Am the One Who Does Not Know How to Ask"

Rabbi Levi Yitzhak of Berditchev said: The Haggadah speaks of four sons: One wise, one wicked, one simple, and one who does not know how to ask. Lord of the world, I, Levi Yitzhak, am the one who does not know how to ask. In such a case, does not the Haggadah say that with the child who does not know how to ask, "You must start with him." The father must take the initiative. Lord of the world, are You not my Father? Am I not Your son? I do not even know what questions to ask. You take the initiative and disclose the answers to me. Show me, in connection with whatever happens to me, what is required of me! What are You asking of me? God, I do not ask You why I suffer. I wish to know only that I suffer for Your sake.

* * *

מַגִּיד

MAGGID, THE NARRATION

Leader

There are many questions. Now we begin to answer.

מֵעַבְדוּת לְחֵרוּת
מִגְּנוּת לְשֶׁבַח
מִמַּלְכוּת הָרִשְׁעָה לְמַלְכוּת שָׁמַיִם

OUR HISTORY MOVES FROM SLAVERY TOWARD FREEDOM.
OUR NARRATION BEGINS WITH DEGRADATION AND RISES TO DIGNITY.
OUR SERVICE OPENS WITH THE RULE OF EVIL AND ADVANCES TOWARD THE KINGDOM OF GOD.

This is our theme:

Group

𝄞 10

עֲבָדִים הָיִינוּ לְפַרְעֹה בְּמִצְרָיִם. וַיּוֹצִיאֵנוּ יְיָ אֱלֹהֵינוּ מִשָּׁם בְּיָד חֲזָקָה וּבִזְרֹעַ נְטוּיָה. וְאִלּוּ לֹא הוֹצִיא הַקָּדוֹשׁ בָּרוּךְ הוּא אֶת־אֲבוֹתֵינוּ מִמִּצְרָיִם. הֲרֵי אָנוּ וּבָנֵינוּ וּבְנֵי בָנֵינוּ מְשֻׁעְבָּדִים הָיִינוּ לְפַרְעֹה בְּמִצְרָיִם.

Physical Servitude

We were slaves to Pharaoh in Egypt, and God freed us from Egypt with a mighty hand. Had not the Holy One, praised be He, delivered our people from Egypt, then we, our children, and our children's children would still be enslaved.

Leader

וַאֲפִילוּ כֻּלָּנוּ חֲכָמִים. כֻּלָּנוּ נְבוֹנִים. כֻּלָּנוּ זְקֵנִים. כֻּלָּנוּ יוֹדְעִים אֶת־הַתּוֹרָה. מִצְוָה עָלֵינוּ לְסַפֵּר בִּיצִיאַת מִצְרָיִם. וְכָל הַמַּרְבֶּה לְסַפֵּר בִּיצִיאַת מִצְרַיִם הֲרֵי זֶה מְשֻׁבָּח:

Therefore, even if
all of us were wise,
all of us people of understanding,
all of us learned in Torah,
it would still be our obligation to tell the story of the Exodus from Egypt. Moreover, whoever searches deeply into its meaning is considered praiseworthy.

Group

For Redemption is not yet complete.

They discussed the going-out from Egypt through the entire Passover night.

מעשה ברבי אליעזר ורבי יהושע ורבי אלעזר בן
עזריה ורבי עקיבא ורבי טרפון שהיו מסבין בבני
ברק. והיו מספרים ביציאת מצרים כל אותו הלילה
עד שבאו תלמידיהם ואמרו להם רבותינו הגיע זמן
קריאת שמע של שחרית.

Leader

מַעֲשֶׂה בְּרַבִּי אֱלִיעֶזֶר וְרַבִּי יְהוֹשֻׁעַ וְרַבִּי אֶלְעָזָר בֶּן עֲזַרְיָה וְרַבִּי עֲקִיבָא וְרַבִּי
טַרְפוֹן שֶׁהָיוּ מְסֻבִּין בִּבְנֵי בְרַק. וְהָיוּ מְסַפְּרִים בִּיצִיאַת מִצְרַיִם כָּל־אוֹתוֹ
הַלַּיְלָה. עַד שֶׁבָּאוּ תַלְמִידֵיהֶם וְאָמְרוּ לָהֶם רַבּוֹתֵינוּ הִגִּיעַ זְמַן קְרִיאַת שְׁמַע
שֶׁל שַׁחֲרִית:

An instance of this is told of Rabbi Eliezer, Rabbi Joshua, Rabbi Elazar the son of Azaria, Rabbi Akiva, and Rabbi Tarphon: At their Seder in B'nai B'rak they discussed the going-out from Egypt through the entire Passover night, until their students came and said to them, "Our teachers, the time has already come to recite the morning Sh'ma!"
(*This Seder took place at a time of rebellion against Roman oppression and the Seder was held in B'nai B'rak, the town of Rabbi Akiva, who was a leader of the revolt.*)

We knew *physical* servitude in Egypt.
But before that, our *souls* were in bondage.

Group

מִתְּחִלָּה עוֹבְדֵי עֲבוֹדָה זָרָה הָיוּ אֲבוֹתֵינוּ וְעַכְשָׁו קֵרְבָנוּ הַמָּקוֹם לַעֲבוֹדָתוֹ.
שֶׁנֶּאֱמַר בְּעֵבֶר הַנָּהָר יָשְׁבוּ אֲבוֹתֵיכֶם מֵעוֹלָם. וַיַּעַבְדוּ אֱלֹהִים אֲחֵרִים:

For in the beginning our ancestors were idolators. But afterward God drew us nearer to His service, as it is written: "Of old your ancestors dwelled beyond the river Euphrates. . . . And they served other gods."

Spiritual Bondage
Joshua 24:2

(*The Seder text continues on page 37.*)

"And They Served Other Gods"

Among the gods worshiped in Mesopotamia, Abraham's birthplace, were:
- The Sky, over-all authority;
- The Storm, violent and powerful;
- The fertile Earth Mother, source of life and sustenance;
- The Water, of sea, river, canals, wells, and procreation.

And in Canaan, the deities were the possessors of the land and the powers of fertility. They were gods of fixed locations who guaranteed the repetition of the established order for the material benefit of their worshiper.

*

According to Erich Fromm, "An idol represents the desire to return to the soil-mother, the craving for possession, power, and fame. The history of mankind up to the present time is primarily the history of idol worship . . . from the primitive idols . . . to the modern idols of the state, the leader, production, and consumption. . . . In worshiping the idol, man worships himself . . . a partial, limited aspect of man; his intelligence, his physical strength, power, fame. . . ."

*

. . . these mortals have set up idols in their mind. . . . They are all turned away from me through their idols.
Ezekiel 14:3–5

*

כְּשֶׁהָיָה אַבְרָהָם בֶּן־שָׁלֹשׁ שָׁנִים יָצָא מִן הַמְּעָרָה, הִרְהֵר בְּלִבּוֹ: מִי בָּרָא שָׁמַיִם וָאָרֶץ וְאוֹתִי? הִתְפַּלֵּל כָּל הַיּוֹם כֻּלּוֹ לַשֶּׁמֶשׁ. לָעֶרֶב שָׁקַע הַשֶּׁמֶשׁ בְּמַעֲרָב וְזָרְחָה הַלְּבָנָה בְּמִזְרָח. כְּשֶׁרָאָה אֶת הַיָּרֵחַ וְכוֹכָבִים סָבִיב לַיָּרֵחַ, אָמַר: זֶה שֶׁבָּרָא הַשָּׁמַיִם וְהָאָרֶץ וְאוֹתִי, וְהַכּוֹכָבִים הַלָּלוּ שָׂרָיו וַעֲבָדָיו. עָמַד כָּל הַלַּיְלָה בִּתְפִלָּה לַיָּרֵחַ. לַבֹּקֶר שָׁקַע הַיָּרֵחַ בְּמַעֲרָב וְזָרַח הַשֶּׁמֶשׁ בְּמִזְרָח. אָמַר: אֵין בְּיַד אֵלּוּ כֹּחַ; אָדוֹן יֵשׁ עֲלֵיהֶם אֵלָיו אֶתְפַּלֵּל וְאֵלָיו אֶשְׁתַּחֲוֶה.

When Abraham was young, he sought to serve the Highest. When the sun sank, and the stars came forth, he said, "These are the gods!" But the dawn came, and the stars could be seen no longer, and then he said, "I will not pay worship to these, for they are no gods." Thereupon the sun came forth, and he spoke, "This is my god; him will I extol." But again the sun set, and he said, "He is no god," and beholding the moon, he called her his god to whom he would pay divine homage. Then the moon was obscured, and he cried out: "This, too, is no god! There is One who sets them all in motion."
Jellinek, Bet Ha-Midrash

*

(On the Sabbath)

To set apart one day a week for freedom, a day on which we would not use the instruments which have been so easily turned into weapons of destruction, a day for being with ourselves, a day of detachment from the vulgar, of independence from external obligations, a day on which we stop worshipping the idols of technical civilization, . . . a day on which handling money is considered a desecration, which man avows his independence of that which is the world's chief idol.
Abraham Joshua Heschel

* * *

Leader

We have known physical bondage and spiritual servitude.
We have also been subjected to *social degradation.*
For in the eyes of others we were a subject people—Arameans.

Group

אֲרַמִּי אֹבֵד אָבִי וַיֵּרֶד מִצְרַיְמָה וַיָּגָר שָׁם בִּמְתֵי מְעָט. וַיְהִי־שָׁם לְגוֹי גָּדוֹל עָצוּם וָרָב.

Social Degradation

Deuteronomy 26:5

My father was a fugitive Aramean. He went down to Egypt with meager numbers and sojourned there, and there became a great and populous nation.

(The Seder text continues on page 38.)

𝕮 "A Great . . . Nation"

מְלַמֵּד שֶׁהָיוּ יִשְׂרָאֵל מְצֻיָּנִים שָׁם

שֶׁלֹּא שִׁנּוּ אֶת שְׁמָם וְלֹא שִׁנּוּ אֶת דָּתָם וּלְשׁוֹנָם בְּכָל הַשָּׁנִים הָרַבּוֹת אֲשֶׁר יָשְׁבוּ שָׁם וְהָיוּ תָּמִיד גּוֹי בִּפְנֵי עַצְמָם, אֻמָּה נִבְדֶּלֶת וְנִפְרֶשֶׁת מֵהַמִּצְרִים וְלֹא נִתְעָרְבוּ בָּהֶם, כְּמוֹ שֶׁיִּקְרֶה לִשְׁאָר עַמִּים, בְּהִתְיַשְּׁבָם יַחַד יִתְעָרְבוּ אֵלּוּ בָּאֵלּוּ, אֲבָל הֵם לֹא שִׁנּוּ שְׁמָם וּלְשׁוֹנָם וְדָתָם וּמַלְבּוּשֵׁיהֶם, וְזֶהוּ „מְצֻיָּנִים". (מכלתא, פסחים)

"A great nation" means it was distinguished in character and tradition. Our people retained its uniqueness in Egypt. They did not alter their way of life, their convictions, their names, their heritage, their faith, their language. By virtue of this self-respect and dignity they merited redemption.

Meḥilta, Pesaḥim: Abarbanel, *Zevaḥ Pesaḥ*

*

True redemption will come to the Jew only if he bears his name and every burden imposed upon him by destiny with gleaming courage and with radiant nobleness which, whether or not they evoke the love of the world without, shall justify the Jew in his own sight and hallow him anew in the Presence of the Eternal to Whom alone he is ultimately accountable.

Rabbi Stephen S. Wise

*

I am a Jew because, born of Israel and having lost her, I have felt her live again in me, more loving than myself.

I am a Jew because, born of Israel and having regained her, I wish her to live after me, more living than myself.

I am a Jew because the faith of Israel demands of me no abdication of the mind.

I am a Jew because the faith of Israel requires of me all the devotion of my heart.

I am a Jew because in every place where suffering weeps, the Jew weeps.

I am a Jew because every time when despair cries out, the Jew hopes.

I am a Jew because the promise of Israel is the universal promise.

I am a Jew because, for Israel, the world is not yet completed: we are completing it.

I am a Jew because for Israel, Humanity is not yet fully formed; humanity must perfect itself.

Edmond Fleg

* * *

Leader

I took your father Abraham from across the river and I led him into the land of Canaan, and I increased his descendants; and I gave him Isaac and to Isaac I gave Jacob. When Jacob and his children went down into Egypt, Joseph was already in Egypt. Joseph had emerged with power over the land of Egypt. . . . There was famine in all lands, but in the

וָאֶקַּח אֶת־אֲבִיכֶם אֶת־אַבְרָהָם מֵעֵבֶר הַנָּהָר וָאוֹלֵךְ אוֹתוֹ בְּכָל־אֶרֶץ כְּנָעַן וָאַרְבֶּה אֶת־זַרְעוֹ וָאֶתֶּן־לוֹ אֶת־יִצְחָק׃ וָאֶתֵּן לְיִצְחָק אֶת־יַעֲקֹב׃ *Joshua 24:3–4*

וַיְהִי כָּל־נֶפֶשׁ יֹצְאֵי יֶרֶךְ־יַעֲקֹב שִׁבְעִים נָפֶשׁ וְיוֹסֵף הָיָה בְמִצְרָיִם׃ *Exodus 1:5*

וַיֵּצֵא יוֹסֵף עַל־אֶרֶץ מִצְרָיִם׃ וַיְהִי רָעָב בְּכָל־הָאֲרָצוֹת וּבְכָל־אֶרֶץ מִצְרַיִם הָיָה לָחֶם׃ וַיֹּאמֶר פַּרְעֹה לְכָל־מִצְרַיִם *Genesis 41:45, 54, 55, 57*

"I took your father Abraham . . ."

לעשות כמה שאמר
לאברהם אבינו
בברית בין
הבתרים. שנאמר. ויאמר לאברם.
ידע תדע כי-גר יהיה זרעך בארץ
לא להם. ועבדום וענו אתם ארבע
מאות שנה: וגם את-הגוי אשר
יעבדו דן אנכי. ואחרי-כן יצאו
ברכש גדול:

ל. באסקין

Exodus 1:6, 8–10

לְכוּ אֶל־יוֹסֵף אֲשֶׁר־יֹאמַר לָכֶם
תַּעֲשׂוּ: וְכָל־הָאָרֶץ בָּאוּ מִצְרַיְמָה
לִשְׁבֹּר אֶל־יוֹסֵף: וַיָּמָת יוֹסֵף וְכָל־
אֶחָיו וְכֹל הַדּוֹר הַהוּא: וַיָּקָם מֶלֶךְ־
חָדָשׁ עַל־מִצְרָיִם אֲשֶׁר לֹא־יָדַע
אֶת־יוֹסֵף: וַיֹּאמֶר אֶל־עַמּוֹ הִנֵּה עַם
בְּנֵי יִשְׂרָאֵל רַב וְעָצוּם מִמֶּנּוּ: הָבָה
נִתְחַכְּמָה לוֹ פֶּן־יִרְבֶּה וְהָיָה כִּי־
תִקְרֶאנָה מִלְחָמָה וְנוֹסַף גַּם־הוּא עַל־
שֹׂנְאֵינוּ וְנִלְחַם־בָּנוּ וְעָלָה מִן־הָאָרֶץ:

land of Egypt, there was bread . . . and Pharaoh said to the Egyptians, "Go to Joseph; whatever he tells you, you shall do" . . . and all the world came to Joseph in Egypt. After Joseph died and all his brothers and all that generation . . . a new king arose over Egypt who did not know Joseph. And he said to his people, "Look, the Israelite people are much too numerous for us. Let us, then, deal shrewdly with them, lest they increase, and in the event of war, join our enemies in fighting against us and gain ascendancy over the country."

"A New King . . ."

וַיָּקָם מֶלֶךְ חָדָשׁ. רַב וּשְׁמוּאֵל. חַד אָמַר חָדָשׁ מַמָּשׁ וְחַד אָמַר שֶׁנִּתְחַדְּשׁוּ גְּזֵרוֹתָיו (סוטה יא): וַאֲשֶׁר לֹא יָדַע. עָשָׂה עַצְמוֹ כְּאִלּוּ לֹא יָדַע:

How was it possible that the "new king" did not know Joseph?
Some commentators explain that he really did not know of Joseph. Others explain that he *acted* as if he did not know Joseph. He willfully closed his eyes to all that the Hebrews had done for Egypt. Led by Pharaoh, those who had formerly honored the Hebrews grew now to despise them.

Rashi, *ad loc.* (based on Talmud Bavli, Sotah 11, the difference of opinion between the great authorities, Rav and Sh'muel)

*

"Let Us, Then, Deal Shrewdly with Them"

We understand from this that Pharaoh had to teach the Egyptians to hate the Hebrews by shrewdly fanning the flames of fear and envy—fear of the growth of the Hebrew settlement and envy of their skill and self-respect.

* * *

Leader

Exodus 1:11, 14, 15

וַיָּשִׂימוּ עָלָיו שָׂרֵי מִסִּים לְמַעַן עַנֹּתוֹ
בְּסִבְלֹתָם וַיִּבֶן עָרֵי מִסְכְּנוֹת לְפַרְעֹה
אֶת־פִּתֹם וְאֶת־רַעַמְסֵס: וַיְמָרְרוּ אֶת־
חַיֵּיהֶם בַּעֲבֹדָה קָשָׁה בְּחֹמֶר וּבִלְבֵנִים
וּבְכָל־עֲבֹדָה בַּשָּׂדֶה וְכַאֲשֶׁר יְעַנּוּ אֹתוֹ
כֵּן יִרְבֶּה וְכֵן יִפְרֹץ וַיָּקֻצוּ מִפְּנֵי בְּנֵי
יִשְׂרָאֵל: וַיְצַו פַּרְעֹה לְכָל־עַמּוֹ לֵאמֹר
כָּל־הַבֵּן הַיִּלּוֹד הַיְאֹרָה תַּשְׁלִיכֻהוּ

So they set taskmasters over them with forced labor and they built garrison cities for Pharaoh: Pithom and Raamses. The Egyptians embittered their lives with harsh labor at mortar and brick and in all sorts of work in the fields. But the more they were oppressed, the more they increased and spread out, so that the Egyptians

וְכָל־הַבֵּט תְּחַיּוּן: וַנִּצְעַק אֶל־יְיָ אֱלֹהֵי אֲבוֹתֵינוּ וַיִּשְׁמַע יְיָ אֶת־קֹלֵנוּ וַיַּרְא אֶת־עָנְיֵנוּ וְאֶת־עֲמָלֵנוּ וְאֶת־לַחֲצֵנוּ.

came to despise and dread the Israelites. So Pharaoh charged all his people, saying, "Every boy that is born shall be thrown in the Nile, but let every girl live." We cried unto יהוה, the God of our ancestors, and God heeded our plight, our misery, and our oppression.

Deuteronomy 26:7

"The Egyptians Embittered Their Lives"

We got used to standing in line at seven o'clock in the morning, at twelve noon, and again at seven o'clock in the evening. We stood in a long queue with a plate in our hand into which they ladled a little warmed-up water with a salty or a coffee flavor. Or else they gave us a few potatoes. We got used to sleeping without a bed, to saluting every uniform, not to walk on the sidewalks, and then again to walk on the sidewalks. We got used to undeserved slaps, blows, and executions. We got accustomed to seeing piled-up coffins full of corpses, to seeing the sick amidst dirt and filth, and to seeing the helpless doctors. We got used to the fact that from time to time, one thousand unhappy souls would come here and that, from time to time, another thousand unhappy souls would go away. . . .

From the prose of fifteen-year-old Peter Fischl, who perished in Auschwitz in 1944

*

"Our Misery"

The "misery" refers, commentators say, to the enforced separation of husbands and wives. Husbands and wives were not allowed to live together. Nevertheless, the women of Israel were a source of strength to their husbands, bringing them food, consoling them when they visited, giving them hope of liberation.

Torah Sh'lema, Sh'mot, ad loc.

*

"Our Oppression"

We are taught that the Egyptians taunted the Israelites for observing the circumcision of their sons. They mocked the Hebrews for this, since the infants were to be put to death anyway. But the Hebrews answered, "We perform our duty; whatever you do later cannot affect our practice of our faith. As our ancestors were faithful to God's covenant, so shall we be."

Seder Eliyahu Rabbah 21

* * *

Leader

Exodus 1:24–25

וַיִּשְׁמַע אֱלֹהִים אֶת־נַאֲקָתָם וַיִּזְכֹּר אֱלֹהִים אֶת־בְּרִיתוֹ אֶת־אַבְרָהָם אֶת־יִצְחָק וְאֶת־יַעֲקֹב: וַיַּרְא אֱלֹהִים אֶת־בְּנֵי יִשְׂרָאֵל וַיֵּדַע אֱלֹהִים:

God heard our moaning,
And God remembered His
Covenant with Abraham, Isaac, and Jacob,
And God looked upon the
Israelites, and God knew. . . .

ויקם מלך חדש

(*The Seder text continues on page 44.*)

"And God Knew. . . ."

Leader

"And God knew. . . ." What did God know?

Group

When the Israelites had grown accustomed to their tasks,
when the Hebrews began to labor without complaint,
then God knew it was time that they be liberated.

Leader

For the worst slavery of Egypt is when we learn to endure it!
"And God knew. . . ."

Group

As long as there was no prospect of freedom,
God knew the Israelites would not awaken to the bitterness of bondage.
First Moses had to teach the taste of freedom's hope,
and only then did servitude taste bitter.

Leader

So though bitter slavery is first, and then comes liberation,
the Seder teaches us to taste the *matzah* of freedom first
and only then the bitter herbs of bondage.
"And God knew. . . ."

Group

"And God knew. . . ." If our freedom had been given us by Pharaoh,
we would have been indebted to him, still subservient,
within ourselves dependent, slavish still at heart. We had to free ourselves!

Leader

And because we freed ourselves, ever after, even when demeaned by others
and suffering privation, within ourselves we always wanted to be free!
"And God knew. . . ."

Group

The God-inspired know that people must aspire to the service of the Highest in order to be free.

Leader

And so our Rabbi of Bratslav taught that others can gain control of you
so long as you possess a will distinct from God's.

Group

And God knew.

* * *

A new king arose over Egypt.

Leader

Exodus 12:12

And God said, "I will go through the land of Egypt on that night . . . and I will mete out justice against all the gods of Egypt. I the Eternal.

And God brought us out of Egypt by a mighty hand, by an outstretched arm and awesome power, and by signs and portents; not through a messenger, not through any intermediary or any supernatural being, but the Holy One, alone, in solitary glory.

שֶׁנֶּאֱמַר: וְעָבַרְתִּי בְאֶרֶץ מִצְרַיִם
בַּלַּיְלָה הַזֶּה, וּבְכָל אֱלֹהֵי מִצְרַיִם
אֶעֱשֶׂה שְׁפָטִים, אֲנִי יְיָ. וַיּוֹצִאֵנוּ יְהוָֹה
מִמִּצְרַיִם בְּיָד חֲזָקָה וּבִזְרֹעַ נְטוּיָה
וּבְמֹרָא גָּדֹל וּבְאֹתוֹת וּבְמֹפְתִים:
לֹא עַל יְדֵי מַלְאָךְ. וְלֹא עַל יְדֵי שָׂרָף.
וְלֹא עַל יְדֵי שָׁלִיחַ. אֶלָּא הַקָּדוֹשׁ בָּרוּךְ
הוּא בִּכְבוֹדוֹ וּבְעַצְמוֹ.

Deuteronomy 26:8

(*The Seder text continues on the next page.*)

Which Is the Way to Redemption?

To Renounce Physical Force?

God alone executed the judgment of death directly by divine power: "For I will go through the land of Egypt in that night. *I and not any intermediary.*" Now obviously, the Holy One, blessed be He, could have given the Children of Israel the power to *avenge themselves* upon the Egyptians, but God did not want to sanction the use of their fists for self-defense even at that time; for, while at that moment they might merely have defended themselves against evil-doers, by such means the way of the fist spreads through the world, and in the end defenders become aggressors. Therefore, the Holy One, blessed be He, took great pains to remove Israel completely from any participation in the vengeance upon the evil-doers, to such an extent that they were not permitted even to see the events.

The children of Israel, then, must derive this lesson from the events of that Passover eve: not to put their trust in wealth, and not to put their trust in might, but rather in the God of truth and justice, for this will serve to defend them everywhere against those who would dominate by the power of the fist.

Rabbi Aaron Samuel Tamaret of Mileitchitz

*

Or to Claim Our Freedom Through Our Own Power?

We are the mighty!
The last generation of slaves and
the first generation of the free!
Alone our hand in its strength
tore from the pride of our shoulders
the yoke of bondage.
We lifted our heads to the heavens,
and behold their broadness was
narrow in the pride of our eyes.

„אֲנַחְנוּ גִּבּוֹרִים!
דּוֹר אַחֲרוֹן לְשִׁעְבּוּד וְרִאשׁוֹן לִגְאֻלָּה
אֲנָחְנוּ!
יָדֵנוּ לְבַדָּהּ, יָדֵנוּ הַחֲזָקָה
אֶת־כֹּבֶד הָעֹל מֵעַל גְּאוֹן צַוָּארֵנוּ
פֵּרְקָה.
וַנִּזְקֹף רֹאשֵׁנוּ שָׁמַיְמָה וַיֵּצְרוּ בְעֵינֵינוּ —

So we turned to the desert, we said
to the Wilderness: "Mother!"
Yea, on the tops of the crags in
the thickness of clouds,
With the eagles of heaven we drank
from her fountains of freedom.

וַנִּפְנֶה לַמִּדְבָּר וַנֹּאמַר לַצִּיָּה "אִמֵּנוּ!"
עַל־רָאשֵׁי הַצּוּרִים בֵּין מִפְלְשֵׂי עָבִים
שָׁתִינוּ מִמְּקוֹרוֹ הַדְּרוֹר עִם כָּל־נִשְׁרֵי
שָׁמַיִם . . . "

Ḥayim Nachman Bialik, translated by Maurice Samuel

* * *

Leader

Exodus 12:40–42 The time the Israelites remained in Egypt was four hundred and thirty years. At the end of the four hundred and thirtieth year, to the very day, all the hosts of God departed from the land of Egypt. That same night is God's watch-night for the children of Israel throughout their generations.

וּמוֹשַׁב בְּנֵי יִשְׂרָאֵל אֲשֶׁר יָשְׁבוּ בְּמִצְרָיִם שְׁלֹשִׁים שָׁנָה וְאַרְבַּע מֵאוֹת שָׁנָה: וַיְהִי מִקֵּץ שְׁלֹשִׁים שָׁנָה וְאַרְבַּע מֵאוֹת שָׁנָה וַיְהִי בְּעֶצֶם הַיּוֹם הַזֶּה יָצְאוּ כָּל־צִבְאוֹת יְהֹוָה מֵאֶרֶץ מִצְרָיִם: לֵיל שִׁמֻּרִים הוּא לַיהֹוָה לְהוֹצִיאָם מֵאֶרֶץ מִצְרָיִם הוּא־הַלַּיְלָה הַזֶּה לַיהֹוָה שִׁמֻּרִים לְכָל־בְּנֵי יִשְׂרָאֵל לְדֹרֹתָם:

(All raise their cups of wine.)

Leader

𝄞 11,12 We praise the God Who keeps faith with the people Israel. God's promise of Redemption in ancient days sustains us now.

בָּרוּךְ שׁוֹמֵר הַבְטָחָתוֹ לְיִשְׂרָאֵל.
בָּרוּךְ הוּא.
וְהִיא שֶׁעָמְדָה לַאֲבוֹתֵינוּ וְלָנוּ

Group

For more than one enemy has risen against us to destroy us. In every generation, in every age, some rise up to plot our annihilation. But a Divine Power sustains and delivers us.

שֶׁלֹּא אֶחָד בִּלְבָד עָמַד עָלֵינוּ לְכַלּוֹתֵינוּ. אֶלָּא שֶׁבְּכָל־דּוֹר וָדוֹר עוֹמְדִים עָלֵינוּ לְכַלּוֹתֵינוּ. וְהַקָּדוֹשׁ בָּרוּךְ הוּא מַצִּילֵנוּ מִיָּדָם:

(All replace their cups untasted.)

(The Seder text continues on page 48.)

"For More Than One Enemy Has Risen Against Us."

That's the difficulty in these times: ideals, dreams, and cherished hopes rise within us, only to meet the horrible truth and be shattered.
It's really a wonder that I haven't dropped all my ideals, because they seem so absurd and impossible to carry out. Yet I keep them, because in spite of every-

thing I still believe that people are really good at heart. I simply can't build up my hopes on a foundation consisting of confusion, misery, and death. I see the world gradually being turned into a wilderness. I hear the ever-approaching thunder, which will destroy us too. I can feel the sufferings of millions and yet, if I look up into the heavens, I think that it will all come right, that this cruelty too will end, and that peace and tranquility will return again.
In the meantime, I must uphold my ideals, for perhaps the time will come when I shall be able to carry them out.

From *The Diary of Anne Frank*

*

In the presence of eyes
which witnessed the slaughter,
which saw the oppression
the heart could not bear,
and as witness the heart
that once taught compassion
until days came to pass
that crushed human feeling,
I have taken an oath: To remember it all,
to remember, not once to forget!
Forget not one thing to the last generation
when degradation shall cease,
to the last, to its ending,
when the rod of instruction
shall have come to conclusion.
An oath: Not in vain passed over
the night of the terror.
An oath: No morning shall see me
  at flesh-pots again.
An oath: Lest from this we learned nothing.

Abraham Shlonsky, "A Vow," translated by Herbert Bronstein. The original poem may be seen in the Yad Va-Shem Holocaust Memorial in Jerusalem and is recited at many S'darim, as a regular practice, in the land of Israel.

*

צי דארף איך פײַערן דעם טאָג פון מײַן געבאָרן –
דאָס זאָלן זאָגן אנדערע – זיי ווייסן בעסער,
נאָר יענע שאָ פון טאָג, ווען כ׳בין באפרײַט געוואָרן
פון הינטער שטעכנדיקן דראָט אין טפיסע־שלעסער,
די שאָ, וואָס אָנגעקומען איז זי אומדערווארט
מיט גליווערדיקן פראָסט אין אָנהייב כוידעש מארט,
באַם הימל אויסגעשטערנטן אינמיטן טאָג,
און מיט דער בראָכע, וואָס איך האָב פון קינדווײַז ניט געזאָגט, –
אָט יענער טאָג ווען ס׳קומט – איך רייד אליין זיך אײַן:
בא יעדן מענטשן־פרײַנט די שאָ וועט יאָמטעוו זײַן,
ניט קלאפנדיק אין טיר צו אים אין שטוב ארײַן.

In every generation, in every age,
some rise up to plot our annihilation.

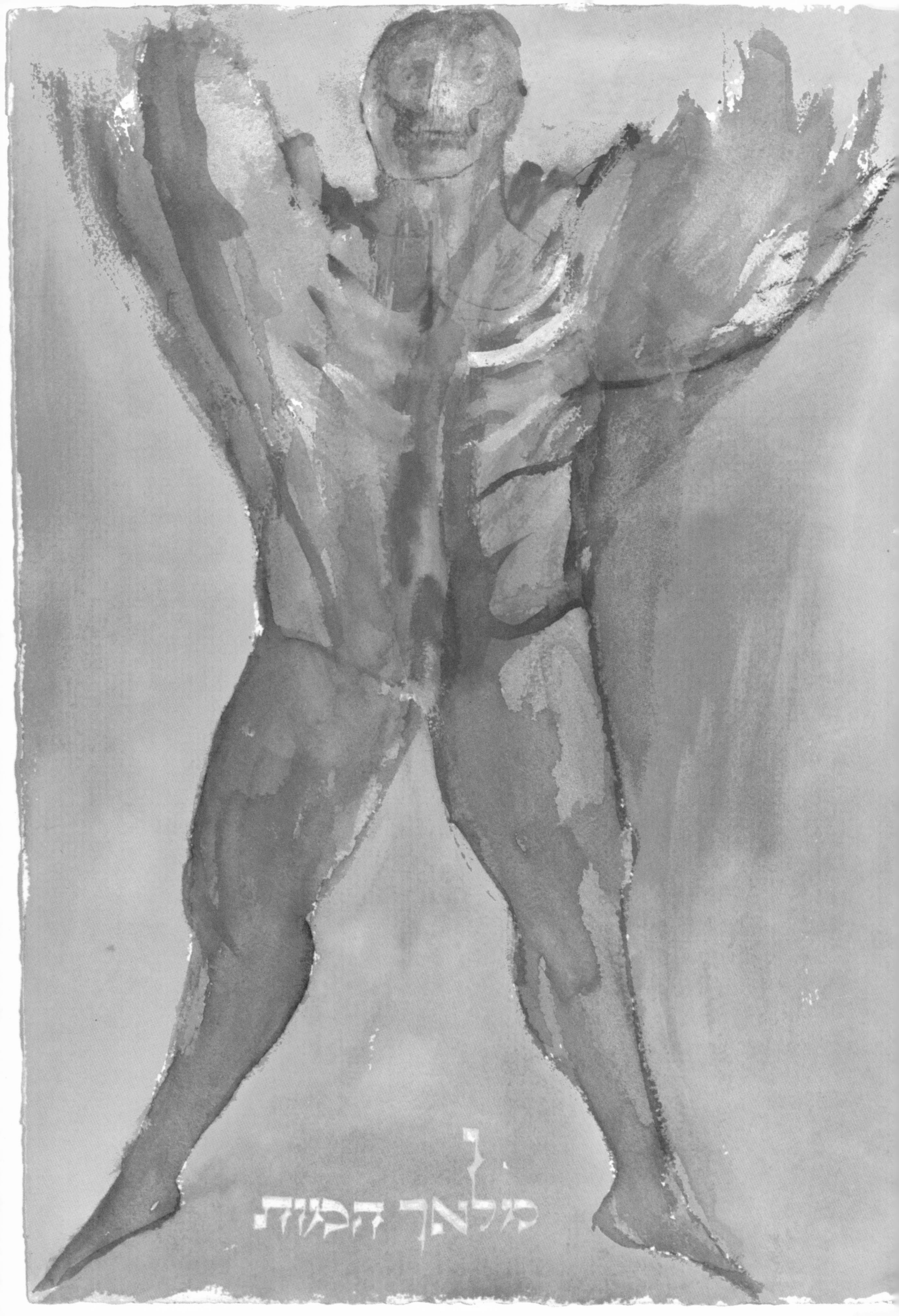
מלאך המות

. . . Only that great moment when they set me free
From barbed-wire fences and the lightless prisons,
That moment suddenly arrived, unguarded,
With early March's glittering frost, and heaven
Lit up with stars at noon, and on my lips
The blessing not said since childhood suddenly
Recalled as if it were but yesterday—
I make myself believe: to every lover
Of humanity that day will be a holiday,
Arriving without asking to come in.

Samuel Halkin, "1959, Russia," translated by Edwin Honig.

*

There have been many, among them Nebuchadnezzar, King of Babylon, and Titus and Vespasian, Emperors of Rome. Yet for all of us who take part in this service, these words, "More than one enemy has risen . . ." are likely to recall with a special and monstrous emphasis what has come to be known to the world as the Holocaust—an explicit program of annihilation of all European Jews, in which six million men, women, and children were efficiently singled out and sent to their deaths. To remember them on this evening, as ones who once shared in this service, is right. Yet we must guard against letting our bitterness at their extermination deflect our hearts from, or diminish our gratitude for, the gift of deliverance that we celebrate tonight. If it is hard for us to understand such vast and barbaric annihilation, it is no easier to understand such a complete and miraculous deliverance as tonight we ritually and jubilantly remember, and seek for in our own lives. Nor are we entitled to judge how such destruction could come to pass. We, as part of the remnant that survived, are entitled only to ask, "Are we among the Saving Remnant? Are we fit for that?" and on this evening, in that hope, to purify our hearts.

Anthony Hecht

* * *

(*"Acts of Redemption" on page* 51 *may be read at this point in place of "The Plagues of Egypt."*)

עֶשֶׂר מַכּוֹת

Makot Mitzrayim, the Plagues of Egypt

Leader

בְּאוֹתָהּ שָׁעָה בִּקְשׁוּ מַלְאֲכֵי־הַשָּׁרֵת לוֹמַר שִׁירָה לִפְנֵי הַקָּדוֹשׁ־בָּרוּךְ־הוּא, אָמַר לָהֶם הַקָּדוֹשׁ־בָּרוּךְ־הוּא: מַעֲשֵׂי יָדַי טוֹבְעִים בַּיָּם וְאַתֶּם אוֹמְרִים שִׁירָה לְפָנָי! (מד׳ אבכיר; סנהד׳ לט:).

Our rabbis taught: When the Egyptian armies were drowning in the sea, the Heavenly Hosts broke out in songs of jubilation. God silenced them and said, "My creatures are perishing, and you sing praises?"

Talmud Bavli, Sanhedrin 39b

Group

Though we descend from those redeemed from brutal Egypt,
and have ourselves rejoiced to see oppressors overcome,
yet our triumph is diminished
by the slaughter of the foe,
as the wine within the cup of joy is lessened
when we pour ten drops for the plagues upon Egypt.

Leader

חֶרֶב בָּאָה לָעוֹלָם, עַל עִנּוּי הַדִּין, וְעַל עִוּוּת הַדִּין.

Pirkei Avot 5:8

Our rabbis taught: "The sword comes into the world because of justice delayed and justice denied."

Group

To remember upheaval that follows oppression,
we pour ten drops for the plagues upon Egypt.

Leader

רַבִּי אוֹמֵר כְּשֵׁם שֶׁהִזְהִיר הַקָּדוֹשׁ בָּרוּךְ הוּא עַל הַדִּבְּרוֹת כַּךְ הִזְהִיר עַל הַדִּין. לָמָּה שֶׁבּוֹ הָעוֹלָם תָּלוּי.

Exodus Rabbah Mishpatim 30:19, 24

Our rabbis taught: God is urgent about justice, for upon justice the world depends. . . .

Group

Each drop of wine we pour is hope and prayer
that people will cast out the plagues that threaten everyone
everywhere they are found, beginning in our own hearts:
The making of war,
the teaching of hate and violence,
despoliation of the earth,
perversion of justice and of government,
fomenting of vice and crime,
neglect of human needs,
oppression of nations and peoples,
corruption of culture,
subjugation of science, learning, and human discourse,
the erosion of freedoms.

אֵלּוּ עֶשֶׂר מַכּוֹת שֶׁהֵבִיא הַקָּדוֹשׁ בָּרוּךְ הוּא עַל־הַמִּצְרִים בְּמִצְרַיִם. וְאֵלּוּ הֵן:

We pour ten drops for the plagues upon Egypt.

צפרדע
ארבה
דם
ברד
דבר
חשך
ערוב
מכת בכורות

Dam, Blood	דָּם.
Tzfardeyah, Frogs	צְפַרְדֵּעַ.
Kinim, Lice	כִּנִּים.
Arov, Wild Beasts	עָרוֹב.
Dever, Blight	דֶּבֶר.
Sh'hin, Boils	שְׁחִין.
Barad, Hail	בָּרָד.
Arbeh, Locusts	אַרְבֶּה.
Hosheh, Darkness	חֹשֶׁךְ.
Makat B'horot, Slaying of the First-Born	מַכַּת בְּכוֹרוֹת:

(*The Seder text continues on page 52.*)

Acts of Redemption

הוֹדוּ לַיהוָֹה קִרְאוּ בִּשְׁמוֹ הוֹדִיעוּ בָעַמִּים עֲלִילוֹתָיו: זִכְרוּ נִפְלְאוֹתָיו אֲשֶׁר־עָשָׂה מֹפְתָיו וּמִשְׁפְּטֵי־פִיו: דִּבְרֵי אֹתוֹתָיו וּמֹפְתִים בְּאֶרֶץ חָם: שָׁלַח חֹשֶׁךְ וַיַּחְשִׁךְ נָתַן גִּשְׁמֵיהֶם בָּרָד אֵשׁ לֶהָבוֹת בְּאַרְצָם: וַיּוֹצִיאֵם בְּכֶסֶף וְזָהָב וְאֵין בִּשְׁבָטָיו כּוֹשֵׁל: פָּרַשׂ עָנָן לְמָסָךְ וְאֵשׁ לְהָאִיר לָיְלָה: וַיִּגְעַר בְּיַם־סוּף וַיֶּחֱרָב וַיּוֹלִיכֵם בַּתְּהֹמוֹת כַּמִּדְבָּר: וַיּוֹשִׁיעֵם מִיַּד שׂוֹנֵא וַיִּגְאָלֵם מִיַּד אוֹיֵב: וַיְכַסּוּ־מַיִם צָרֵיהֶם כִּי זָכַר אֶת־דְּבַר קָדְשׁוֹ אֶת־אַבְרָהָם עַבְדּוֹ: וַיּוֹצִא עַמּוֹ בְשָׂשׂוֹן בְּרִנָּה אֶת־בְּחִירָיו: וַיַּאֲמִינוּ בִדְבָרָיו יָשִׁירוּ תְּהִלָּתוֹ:

Acknowledge יהוה. Call out His name.
Make known among the people His mighty acts. . . .
Remember the wonders which He wrought,
The marvels, the judgments of His mouth . . .
His manifold signs and marvels in the land of Ham.
He sent darkness and it became dark,
For their rain He gave them hail,
Flaming fire throughout their land.
And He brought forth His people. . . .
Among His tribes none failed. . . .
For them He spread forth a cloud as a protective covering
And fire to light the way for them at night. . . .
And He rebuked the Red Sea, and it was dried up;
And He led them through the depths, as through a wilderness.
And He saved them from the hand of him that hated them,
And redeemed them from the hand of the enemy.
And the waters covered their adversaries;
For He remembered His holy word
Unto Abraham His servant;
And He brought forth His people with joy,
His chosen ones with singing.
Then believed they His words;
They sang His praise.

From Psalm 105

* * *

The plagues of Egypt.

Leader

מִי־כָמֹכָה בָּאֵלִם יְהֹוָה. מִי כָּמֹכָה נֶאְדָּר בַּקֹּדֶשׁ נוֹרָא תְהִלֹּת עֹשֵׂה־פֶלֶא: יְהֹוָה יִמְלֹךְ לְעֹלָם וָעֶד:

Who is like unto You, O God, among the Mighty! *Exodus 15:11*
Who is like unto You, awesome in praises, working wonders!
יהוה shall reign forever and ever!

כַּמָּה מַעֲלוֹת טוֹבוֹת לַמָּקוֹם עָלֵינוּ:

How many gifts God has bestowed upon us!

אִלּוּ הוֹצִיאָנוּ מִמִּצְרַיִם. 𝄞 13
וְלֹא קָרַע לָנוּ אֶת הַיָּם. דַּיֵּנוּ:
אִלּוּ קָרַע לָנוּ אֶת הַיָּם.
וְלֹא הֶעֱבִירָנוּ בְתוֹכוֹ בֶּחָרָבָה דַּיֵּנוּ:
אִלּוּ הֶעֱבִירָנוּ בְתוֹכוֹ בֶּחָרָבָה.
וְלֹא סִפֵּק צָרְכֵּנוּ בַּמִּדְבָּר אַרְבָּעִים שָׁנָה דַּיֵּנוּ:
אִלּוּ סִפֵּק צָרְכֵּנוּ בַּמִּדְבָּר אַרְבָּעִים שָׁנָה
וְלֹא הֶאֱכִילָנוּ אֶת־הַמָּן דַּיֵּנוּ:
אִלּוּ הֶאֱכִילָנוּ אֶת־הַמָּן.
וְלֹא נָתַן לָנוּ אֶת־הַשַּׁבָּת. דַּיֵּנוּ:
אִלּוּ נָתַן לָנוּ אֶת־הַשַּׁבָּת.
וְלֹא קֵרְבָנוּ לִפְנֵי הַר סִינַי דַּיֵּנוּ:
אִלּוּ קֵרְבָנוּ לִפְנֵי הַר סִינַי.
וְלֹא נָתַן לָנוּ אֶת־הַתּוֹרָה דַּיֵּנוּ:
אִלּוּ נָתַן לָנוּ אֶת־הַתּוֹרָה.
וְלֹא הִכְנִיסָנוּ לְאֶרֶץ יִשְׂרָאֵל דַּיֵּנוּ:
אִלּוּ הִכְנִיסָנוּ לְאֶרֶץ יִשְׂרָאֵל.
וְלֹא בָנָה לָנוּ אֶת־בֵּית הַבְּחִירָה דַּיֵּנוּ:
אִלּוּ בָנָה לָנוּ אֶת־בֵּית הַבְּחִירָה
וְלֹא שָׁלַח אֵלֵינוּ נְבִיאֵי הָאֱמֶת. דַּיֵּנוּ:
אִלּוּ שָׁלַח אֵלֵינוּ נְבִיאֵי הָאֱמֶת.
וְלֹא שָׂמָנוּ לְעַם קָדוֹשׁ. דַּיֵּנוּ:

Had God brought us out of Egypt and not divided the sea for us, Dayeinu!

Had God divided the sea and not permitted us to cross on dry land, Dayeinu!

Had God permitted us to cross the sea on dry land and not sustained us for forty years in the desert, Dayeinu!

Had God sustained us for forty years in the desert and not fed us with manna, Dayeinu!

Had God fed us with manna and not given us the Sabbath,
Dayeinu!
Had God given us the Sabbath and not brought us to Mount Sinai,
Dayeinu!
Had God brought us to Mount Sinai and not given us the Torah,
Dayeinu!
Had God given us the Torah and not led us into the land of Israel,
Dayeinu!
Had God led us into the land of Israel and not built for us the Temple,
Dayeinu!
Had God built for us the Temple and not sent us prophets of truth,
Dayeinu!
Had God sent us prophets of truth and not made us a holy people,
Dayeinu!

עַל אַחַת כַּמָּה וְכַמָּה טוֹבָה כְפוּלָה וּמְכֻפֶּלֶת לַמָּקוֹם עָלֵינוּ. שֶׁהוֹצִיאָנוּ מִמִּצְרָיִם. וְקָרַע לָנוּ אֶת הַיָּם. וְהֶעֱבִירָנוּ בְתוֹכוֹ בֶּחָרָבָה. וְסִפֵּק צָרְכֵּנוּ בַּמִּדְבָּר אַרְבָּעִים שָׁנָה. וְהֶאֱכִילָנוּ אֶת־הַמָּן. וְנָתַן לָנוּ אֶת־הַשַּׁבָּת. וְקֵרְבָנוּ לִפְנֵי הַר סִינַי. וְנָתַן לָנוּ אֶת־הַתּוֹרָה. וְהִכְנִיסָנוּ לְאֶרֶץ יִשְׂרָאֵל. וּבָנָה לָנוּ אֶת־בֵּית הַבְּחִירָה. וְשָׁלַח אֵלֵינוּ נְבִיאֵי הָאֱמֶת. וְשָׂמָנוּ לְעַם קָדוֹשׁ לְתַקֵּן עוֹלָם בְּמַלְכוּת שַׁדַּי בֶּאֱמֶת וּבִצְדָקָה.

How plentiful are the reasons for our gratitude to God for the many favors bestowed upon us! God brought us out of Egypt, divided the Red Sea for us, permitted us to cross on dry land, sustained us for forty years in the desert, fed us with manna, ordained the Sabbath, brought us to Mount Sinai, gave us the Torah, led us into the land of Israel, built for us the Temple, sent us prophets of truth, and made us a holy people to perfect the world under the kingdom of the Almighty, in truth and in righteousness.

Leader

רַבָּן גַּמְלִיאֵל הָיָה אוֹמֵר. כָּל־שֶׁלֹּא אָמַר שְׁלֹשָׁה דְבָרִים אֵלּוּ בַּפֶּסַח לֹא יָצָא יְדֵי חוֹבָתוֹ. וְאֵלּוּ הֵן. פֶּסַח מַצָּה וּמָרוֹר:

Pesahim 10:5

According to the Mishnah, Rabbi Gamliel said: Whoever does not consider well the meaning of these three, *pesaḥ*, *matzah*, *maror*, has not fulfilled the purpose of the Seder.

(*The leader points to the* z'roah *or shankbone.*)

פֶּסַח שֶׁהָיוּ אֲבוֹתֵינוּ אוֹכְלִין בִּזְמַן שֶׁבֵּית הַמִּקְדָּשׁ קַיָּם. עַל שׁוּם מָה.

What is the meaning of this *pesaḥ*?

אלו קרבנו לפני הר סיני. ולא נתן לנו את התורה דיינו

A Participant

עַל שׁוּם שֶׁפָּסַח הַקָּדוֹשׁ בָּרוּךְ הוּא עַל בָּתֵּי אֲבוֹתֵינוּ בְּמִצְרָיִם. בְּנָגְפּוֹ אֶת־מִצְרָיִם.

In family groups, our people ate the paschal lamb when the Temple was still standing. For them, the *pesaḥ* was a reminder that God "passed over" (*pasaḥ*) the houses of our ancestors in Egypt during the redemption.

Group

In our day, too, we invoke God as the guardian of the household of Israel, as in our dwellings we renew the family bond and strengthen our ties with the whole household of Israel.

(*The leader points to the* matzah.)

Leader

מַצָּה זוֹ שֶׁאָנוּ אוֹכְלִים עַל שׁוּם מָה.

What is the meaning of this *matzah*?

A Participant

עַל שׁוּם שֶׁלֹּא הִסְפִּיק בְּצֵקָם שֶׁל אֲבוֹתֵינוּ לְהַחֲמִיץ: שֶׁנֶּאֱמַר וַיֹּאפוּ אֶת־הַבָּצֵק אֲשֶׁר הוֹצִיאוּ מִמִּצְרַיִם עֻגֹת מַצּוֹת כִּי לֹא חָמֵץ כִּי־גֹרְשׁוּ מִמִּצְרַיִם וְלֹא יָכְלוּ לְהִתְמַהְמֵהַּ וְגַם־צֵדָה לֹא עָשׂוּ לָהֶם:

Of old, *matzah* was meant to recall that the dough prepared by our people had no time to rise before the final act of Redemption. "And they baked unleavened cakes of the dough since they had been driven out of Egypt and could not delay, nor had they prepared provisions for themselves."

Exodus 12:39

Group

To the driven of the earth we link ourselves today as we fulfill the *mitzvah*: "For seven days shall you eat *matzah*, that you may remember your departure from Egypt as long as you live."

Deuteronomy 16:3

(*The leader points to the* maror.)

Leader

מָרוֹר זֶה שֶׁאָנוּ אוֹכְלִים עַל שׁוּם מָה.

What is the meaning of this *maror*?

A Participant

עַל שׁוּם שֶׁמֵּרְרוּ הַמִּצְרִיִּים אֶת־חַיֵּי אֲבוֹתֵינוּ בְּמִצְרָיִם. שֶׁנֶּאֱמַר וַיְמָרְרוּ אֶת־

חַיֵּיהֶם בַּעֲבֹדָה קָשָׁה בְּחֹמֶר וּבִלְבֵנִים וּבְכָל־עֲבֹדָה בַּשָּׂדֶה אֵת כָּל־עֲבֹדָתָם
אֲשֶׁר־עָבְדוּ בָהֶם בְּפָרֶךְ:

It was eaten, they said, because the Egyptians embittered the lives of our people, as it is written: "With hard labor at mortar and brick and in all sorts of work in the field, with all the tasks ruthlessly imposed upon them." *Exodus 1:14*

Group

Today, as well, wherever slavery remains, Jews taste its bitterness.

(*"Pesaḥ Time" may be sung at this point, should it be helpful for the amusement and interest of children present.*) 𝄞 14

Leader

בְּכָל דּוֹר וָדוֹר חַיָּב אָדָם לִרְאוֹת אֶת־עַצְמוֹ כְּאִלּוּ הוּא יָצָא מִמִּצְרָיִם. שֶׁנֶּאֱמַר
וְהִגַּדְתָּ לְבִנְךָ בַּיּוֹם הַהוּא לֵאמֹר בַּעֲבוּר זֶה עָשָׂה יְיָ לִי בְּצֵאתִי מִמִּצְרָיִם:

In every generation, each of us should feel as though we ourselves had gone forth from Egypt, as it is written: "And you shall explain to your child on that day, it is because of what the Eternal did for me when I, *myself*, went forth from Egypt." *Exodus 13:8*

Group

Still we remember: "It was we who were slaves, . . . we who were strangers." And therefore, we recall these words as well:

Leader

You shall not oppress a stranger, for you know the feelings of the stranger, *Exodus 23:9*

Group

וְגֵר לֹא תִלְחָץ וְאַתֶּם יְדַעְתֶּם אֶת־נֶפֶשׁ הַגֵּר כִּי־גֵרִים הֱיִיתֶם בְּאֶרֶץ מִצְרָיִם:

having yourselves been strangers in the land of Egypt.

Leader

When strangers reside with you in your land, you shall not wrong them. . . . You shall love them as yourself, *Leviticus 19:33–34*

Group

וַאֲהַבְתֶּם אֶת־הַגֵּר כִּי־גֵרִים הֱיִיתֶם בְּאֶרֶץ מִצְרָיִם:

for you were strangers in the land of Egypt.

Leader

Deuteronomy 16:11

You shall rejoice before God with your son and daughter . . . and the stranger, and the orphan, and the widow in your midst.

Group

וְשָׂמַחְתָּ לִפְנֵי יְהוָה אֱלֹהֶיךָ אַתָּה וּבִנְךָ וּבִתֶּךָ וְהַגֵּר וְהַיָּתוֹם וְהָאַלְמָנָה אֲשֶׁר
בְּקִרְבֶּךָ׃ וְזָכַרְתָּ כִּי־עֶבֶד הָיִיתָ בְּמִצְרָיִם׃

Deuteronomy 16:12

Always remember that you were slaves in the land of Egypt.

Leader

You shall not subvert the rights of the stranger or the orphan.

Group

לֹא תַטֶּה מִשְׁפַּט גֵּר יָתוֹם וְזָכַרְתָּ כִּי עֶבֶד הָיִיתָ בְּמִצְרָיִם׃

Deuteronomy 24:17–18

Remember that you were a slave in the land of Egypt.

Leader

לֹא אֶת־אֲבוֹתֵינוּ בִּלְבָד גָּאַל הַקָּדוֹשׁ בָּרוּךְ הוּא. אֶלָּא אַף אוֹתָנוּ גָּאַל עִמָּהֶם.
שֶׁנֶּאֱמַר וְאוֹתָנוּ הוֹצִיא מִשָּׁם לְמַעַן הָבִיא אֹתָנוּ לָתֶת לָנוּ אֶת־הָאָרֶץ אֲשֶׁר נִשְׁבַּע
לַאֲבֹתֵינוּ׃

Deuteronomy 6:23

Not only our ancestors alone did the Holy One redeem but *us* as well, along with them, as it is written: "And God freed *us* from Egypt so as to take us and give us the land sworn to our ancestors."

(*The wine cups are raised.*)

𝄞 15

לְפִיכָךְ אֲנַחְנוּ חַיָּבִים לְהוֹדוֹת לְהַלֵּל לְשַׁבֵּחַ לְפָאֵר לְרוֹמֵם לְהַדֵּר לְבָרֵךְ לְעַלֵּה
וּלְקַלֵּס לְמִי שֶׁעָשָׂה לַאֲבוֹתֵינוּ וְלָנוּ אֶת־כָּל־הַנִּסִּים הָאֵלֶּה. הוֹצִיאָנוּ מֵעַבְדוּת
לְחֵרוּת. מִיָּגוֹן לְשִׂמְחָה. מֵאֵבֶל לְיוֹם טוֹב. וּמֵאֲפֵלָה לְאוֹר גָּדוֹל. וּמִשִּׁעְבּוּד
לִגְאֻלָּה. וְנֹאמַר לְפָנָיו שִׁירָה חֲדָשָׁה: הַלְלוּיָהּ.

Therefore, let us rejoice
At the wonder of our deliverance
   From bondage to freedom,
   From agony to joy,
   From mourning to festivity,
   From darkness to light,
   From servitude to redemption.
Before God let us ever sing a new song.

(*The wine cups are set down. Read one or both of the following psalms.*)

מרור

זה שאנו אוכלים על שום מה

על שום שמררו המצרים
את חיי אבותינו במצרים
שנאמר וימררו את חייהם
בעבודה קשה בחמר ובלבנים ובכל
עבודה בשדה את כל עבדתם אשר
עבדו בהם בפרך:

𝄞 16,17

הַלְלוּיָהּ
הַלְלוּ עַבְדֵי יְיָ. הַלְלוּ אֶת־שֵׁם יְיָ:
יְהִי שֵׁם יְיָ מְבֹרָךְ מֵעַתָּה וְעַד עוֹלָם:
מִמִּזְרַח־שֶׁמֶשׁ עַד־מְבוֹאוֹ מְהֻלָּל שֵׁם יְיָ:
רָם עַל־כָּל־גּוֹיִם יְיָ עַל־הַשָּׁמַיִם כְּבוֹדוֹ:
מִי כַּייָ אֱלֹהֵינוּ הַמַּגְבִּיהִי לָשָׁבֶת:
הַמַּשְׁפִּילִי לִרְאוֹת בַּשָּׁמַיִם וּבָאָרֶץ:
מְקִימִי מֵעָפָר דָּל מֵאַשְׁפּוֹת יָרִים אֶבְיוֹן:
לְהוֹשִׁיבִי עִם־נְדִיבִים עִם נְדִיבֵי עַמּוֹ:
מוֹשִׁיבִי עֲקֶרֶת הַבַּיִת אֵם־הַבָּנִים שְׂמֵחָה הַלְלוּיָהּ:

Psalm 113

Halleluyah.
Praise, O servants of **יהוה**,
Praise the name of **יהוה**!
God's name is praised in every place
From where the sun rises to where it sets.
God is exalted above all nations,
His glory is beyond all heavens.
Who is like **יהוה** our God,
Whose throne is set on High
But lowers His gaze to heaven and earth,
Raising the poor from the dust,
Lifting the destitute from the squalor,
Seating them among nobility
With the princely of their people,
Changing the barren woman
To a joyful mother of children . . .
Halleluyah.

*

𝄞 18,19

בְּצֵאת יִשְׂרָאֵל מִמִּצְרָיִם בֵּית יַעֲקֹב מֵעַם לֹעֵז:
הָיְתָה יְהוּדָה לְקָדְשׁוֹ יִשְׂרָאֵל מַמְשְׁלוֹתָיו:
הַיָּם רָאָה וַיָּנֹס הַיַּרְדֵּן יִסֹּב לְאָחוֹר:
הֶהָרִים רָקְדוּ כְאֵילִים גְּבָעוֹת כִּבְנֵי־צֹאן:
מַה־לְּךָ הַיָּם כִּי תָנוּס הַיַּרְדֵּן תִּסֹּב לְאָחוֹר:
הֶהָרִים תִּרְקְדוּ כְאֵילִים גְּבָעוֹת כִּבְנֵי־צֹאן:
מִלִּפְנֵי אָדוֹן חוּלִי אָרֶץ מִלִּפְנֵי אֱלוֹהַּ יַעֲקֹב:
הַהֹפְכִי הַצּוּר אֲגַם־מָיִם חַלָּמִישׁ לְמַעְיְנוֹ־מָיִם:

Psalm 114

When Israel went forth from Egypt,
Jacob's house from the alien nation,

The Egyptians embittered the lives of our people.

Then Judah became His holy place,
Israel His dominion. . . .
Tremble, O earth,
At the presence of the Lord,
At the presence of the God of Jacob,
Who turns the rocks into pools,
The flint into fountains.

כּוֹס גְאוּלָּה

Kos G'ulah, the Second Cup—the Cup of Redemption

Leader

With the second cup of wine we recall the second promise of liberation:

Group

שֶׁנֶּאֱמַר וְהִצַּלְתִּי אֶתְכֶם מֵעֲבֹדָתָם.

As it is written: "*I will deliver you* from their bondage. . . ." *Exodus 6:6*

בָּרוּךְ אַתָּה, יְיָ אֱלֹהֵינוּ, מֶלֶךְ הָעוֹלָם, אֲשֶׁר גְּאָלָנוּ וְגָאַל אֶת אֲבוֹתֵינוּ מִמִּצְרַיִם, וְהִגִּיעָנוּ לַלַּיְלָה הַזֶּה, לֶאֱכָל־בּוֹ מַצָּה וּמָרוֹר. כֵּן, יְיָ אֱלֹהֵינוּ וֵאלֹהֵי אֲבוֹתֵינוּ, יַגִּיעֵנוּ לְמוֹעֲדִים וְלִרְגָלִים אֲחֵרִים, הַבָּאִים לִקְרָאתֵנוּ לְשָׁלוֹם, שְׂמֵחִים בְּבִנְיַן עִירֶךָ, וְשָׂשִׂים בַּעֲבוֹדָתֶךָ. בָּרוּךְ אַתָּה, יְיָ, גָּאַל יִשְׂרָאֵל.

Remembering with gratitude the redemption of our ancestors from Egypt,
rejoicing in the fruits of our struggle for freedom,
we look now with hope to the celebration of a future redemption,
the building of the City of Peace in which all will rejoice
in the service of God, singing together a new song.
We praise Thee, O God, Redeemer of Israel!

בָּרוּךְ אַתָּה יְיָ אֱלֹהֵינוּ מֶלֶךְ הָעוֹלָם בּוֹרֵא פְּרִי הַגָּפֶן:

Baruḥ Atah Adonai Eloheinu Meleḥ ha-olam borei p'ri ha-gafen.

We praise Thee, O God, Sovereign of all existence, Who creates the fruit of the vine[c]

(All drink the second cup of wine.)

(Those who deferred the reading of the "Motzi" *and* "Koreḥ" *sections on page 28 should read them here.)*

שֻׁלְחָן עוֹרֵךְ

SHULḤAN OREIḤ, THE MEAL IS SERVED

It is customary to begin the meal with hard-boiled eggs flavored with salt water. This was the practice in Roman times. The egg has come to be symbolic of new growth, of new life, of hope. The roasted egg on the Seder plate has come to represent the ancient Temple service in Jerusalem, the holy city.

צָפוּן

TZAFUN, THE SEARCH FOR THE HIDDEN

Toward the end of the meal, the children look for the afikoman, *which the leader has hidden. Since neither the meal nor the Seder can be concluded before some of the group has eaten a piece of it, whoever finds the* afikoman *may demand a reward. Nothing is eaten after the* afikoman, *so that the* matzah *may be the last food tasted.*

The afikoman *replaces the "after-dinner entertainment"* (epikomios), *an aspect of the ancient Roman feast that the rabbis eliminated from the Seder so that the entire evening might be devoted only to the observance of Passover. Yet song and festivity remain a part of the Seder feast, including some planned merriment for the children, appropriate to the service.*

בָּרֵךְ

BAREIḤ, THANKS FOR DIVINE SUSTENANCE

(*After the* afikoman *is shared, the service resumes with the* Birkat Hamazon. *A complete Hebrew text is found on pages 65–67.*)

𝄞 20

שִׁיר הַמַּעֲלוֹת בְּשׁוּב יְהוָֹה אֶת־שִׁיבַת צִיּוֹן הָיִינוּ כְּחֹלְמִים: אָז יִמָּלֵא שְׂחוֹק פִּינוּ
וּלְשׁוֹנֵנוּ רִנָּה אָז יֹאמְרוּ בַגּוֹיִם הִגְדִּיל יְהוָֹה לַעֲשׂוֹת עִם־אֵלֶּה: הִגְדִּיל יְהוָֹה
לַעֲשׂוֹת עִמָּנוּ הָיִינוּ שְׂמֵחִים: שׁוּבָה יְהוָֹה אֶת־שְׁבִיתֵנוּ כַּאֲפִיקִים בַּנֶּגֶב: הַזֹּרְעִים
בְּדִמְעָה בְּרִנָּה יִקְצֹרוּ: הָלוֹךְ יֵלֵךְ וּבָכֹה נֹשֵׂא מֶשֶׁךְ־הַזָּרַע בֹּא־יָבוֹא בְרִנָּה
נֹשֵׂא אֲלֻמֹּתָיו:

Psalm 126

A Song of Ascent:

When God restores the exiled of Zion,
We shall be as those who dream.
Our mouths will be full of laughter then,
Our tongues with song.

Then will they say among the nations:
"God has done great things for them."
God has done great things for us,
And so we now rejoice.
Restore us once again, O God,
Like sudden floodstreams in the desert.
Then those who sow in tears,
Will reap in joy.
Those who go forth weeping
Bearing the seed for sowing
Will return bearing the sheaves,
With song and with laughter.

Leader

רַבּוֹתַי נְבָרֵךְ 𝄞 21

Friends, let us say Grace.

Group

יְהִי שֵׁם יְיָ מְבֹרָךְ מֵעַתָּה וְעַד־עוֹלָם:

The name of the Eternal be blessed from now unto eternity.

Leader

בִּרְשׁוּת מָרָנָן וְרַבָּנָן וְרַבּוֹתַי נְבָרֵךְ אֱלֹהֵינוּ שֶׁאָכַלְנוּ מִשֶּׁלּוֹ:

Let us praise God of Whose bounty we have partaken.

Group

בָּרוּךְ אֱלֹהֵינוּ שֶׁאָכַלְנוּ מִשֶּׁלּוֹ וּבְטוּבוֹ חָיִינוּ:

Let us praise our God of Whose bounty we have
partaken and by Whose goodness we live.

בָּרוּךְ הוּא וּבָרוּךְ שְׁמוֹ:

בָּרוּךְ אַתָּה יְיָ אֱלֹהֵינוּ מֶלֶךְ הָעוֹלָם, הַזָּן אֶת־הָעוֹלָם כֻּלּוֹ בְּטוּבוֹ בְּחֵן בְּחֶסֶד וּבְרַחֲמִים הוּא נוֹתֵן לֶחֶם לְכָל־בָּשָׂר כִּי לְעוֹלָם חַסְדּוֹ: וּבְטוּבוֹ הַגָּדוֹל תָּמִיד לֹא חָסַר־לָנוּ וְאַל יֶחְסַר־לָנוּ מָזוֹן לְעוֹלָם וָעֶד בַּעֲבוּר שְׁמוֹ הַגָּדוֹל: כִּי הוּא אֵל זָן וּמְפַרְנֵס לַכֹּל וּמֵטִיב לַכֹּל וּמֵכִין מָזוֹן לְכָל־בְּרִיּוֹתָיו אֲשֶׁר בָּרָא. בָּרוּךְ אַתָּה יְיָ, הַזָּן אֶת־הַכֹּל:

Through God's kindness, mercy, and compassion,
all existence is eternally sustained.
God is forever faithful.
Surpassing goodness fills all time and space.

Therefore, let us rejoice
at the wonder of our deliverance.

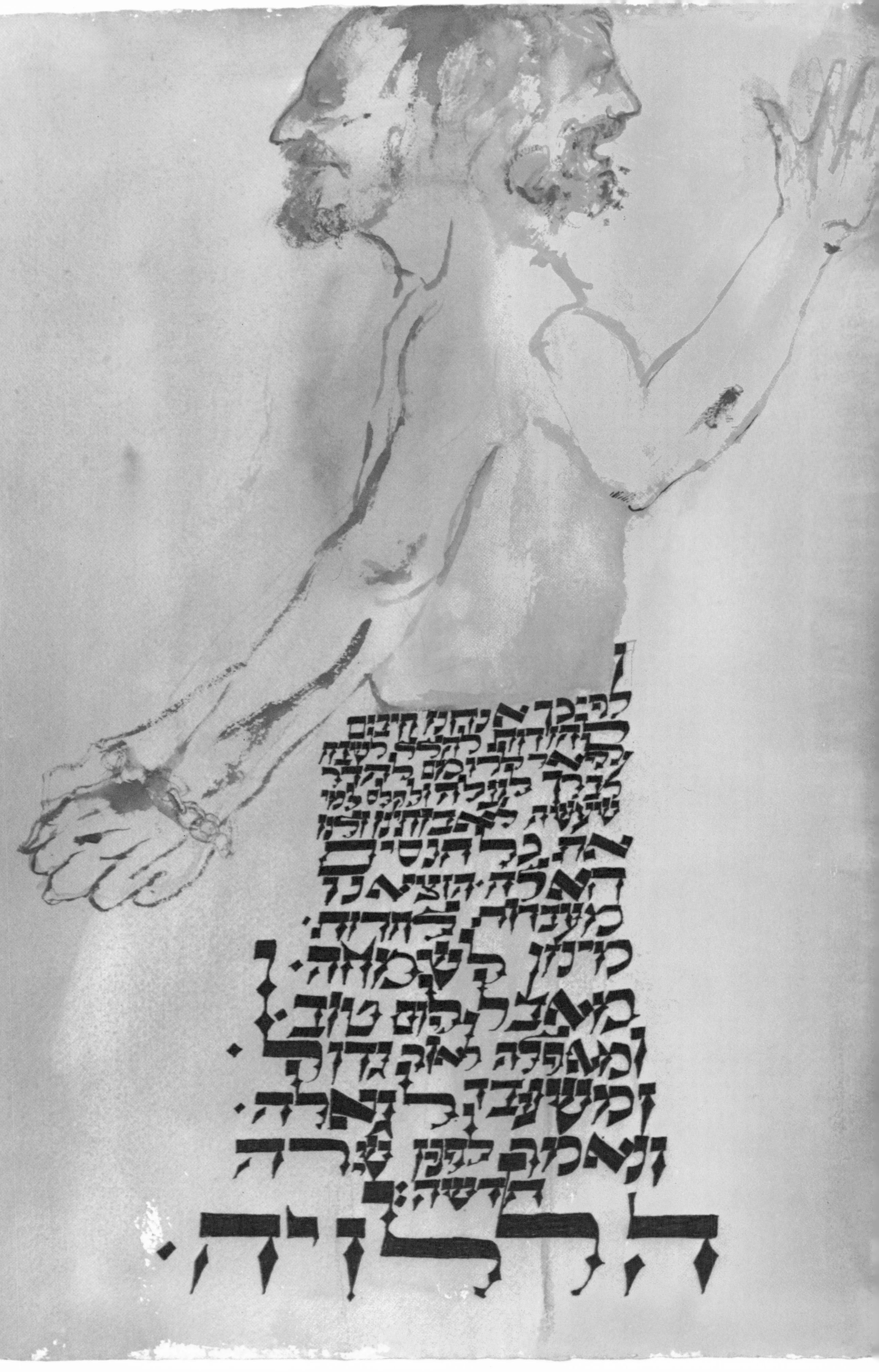
לפיכך אנחנו חייבים
להודות להלל לשבח
לפאר לרומם להדר
לברך לעלה ולקלס למי
שעשה לאבותינו ולנו
את כל הנסים
האלה הוציאנו
מעבדות לחרות
מיגון לשמחה
ומאבל ליום טוב
ומאפלה לאור גדול
ומשעבוד לגאלה
ונאמר לפניו שירה
חדשה
הללויה

Sustenance there is for all.
None need ever lack,
no being ever want for food.
We praise our God, the One, sustaining all.

וּבְנֵה יְרוּשָׁלַיִם עִיר הַקֹּדֶשׁ בִּמְהֵרָה בְיָמֵינוּ. בָּרוּךְ אַתָּה יְיָ בּוֹנֵה בְרַחֲמָיו יְרוּשָׁלָיִם. אָמֵן:

And build Jerusalem, O God, speedily in our days. We praise our God Whose compassion ever builds Jerusalem.

Leader

בְּיוֹם חַג הַמַּצּוֹת הַזֶּה זָכְרֵנוּ יְיָ אֱלֹהֵינוּ בּוֹ לְטוֹבָה.

On this Festival of *Matzot*, inspire us to goodness.

Group

וּפָקְדֵנוּ בוֹ לִבְרָכָה.

On this Day of Liberation, make us a blessing.

Leader

וְהוֹשִׁיעֵנוּ בוֹ לְחַיִּים.

On this Festival of *Pesaḥ*, preserve us in life.

Group

הָרַחֲמָן. הוּא יִמְלוֹךְ עָלֵינוּ לְעוֹלָם וָעֶד:

All Merciful, rule over us forever.

Leader

הָרַחֲמָן. הוּא יְפַרְנְסֵנוּ בְּכָבוֹד:

Sustain us with honorable work.

Leader

(On the Sabbath include the following:)

הָרַחֲמָן. הוּא יַנְחִילֵנוּ יוֹם שֶׁכֻּלּוֹ שַׁבָּת וּמְנוּחָה לְחַיֵּי הָעוֹלָמִים:

All Merciful, may we inherit
a Sabbath of eternal peace.

(On weekdays continue here:)

הָרַחֲמָן. הוּא יְזַכֵּנוּ לִימוֹת הַמָּשִׁיחַ וּלְחַיֵּי הָעוֹלָם הַבָּא:

Make us worthy of the Messianic promise
of a world that is yet to be.

Group

הָרַחֲמָן. הוּא יִשְׁלַח בְּרָכָה מְרֻבָּה בַּבַּיִת הַזֶּה וְעַל שֻׁלְחָן זֶה שֶׁאָכַלְנוּ עָלָיו:
הָרַחֲמָן. הוּא יְבָרֵךְ אוֹתָנוּ וְאֶת כָּל־אֲשֶׁר לָנוּ, כְּמוֹ שֶׁנִּתְבָּרְכוּ אֲבוֹתֵינוּ אַבְרָהָם יִצְחָק וְיַעֲקֹב בַּכֹּל מִכֹּל כֹּל, כֵּן יְבָרֵךְ אוֹתָנוּ כֻּלָּנוּ יַחַד בִּבְרָכָה שְׁלֵמָה. וְנֹאמַר אָמֵן:

May the One Who blessed Abraham, Isaac, and Jacob,
May the One Who blessed our Mothers,
bless this house, this table, and all assembled here;
and so may all our loved ones share our blessing.

Leader

עֹשֶׂה שָׁלוֹם בִּמְרוֹמָיו הוּא יַעֲשֶׂה שָׁלוֹם עָלֵינוּ וְעַל כָּל־יִשְׂרָאֵל. וְאִמְרוּ אָמֵן:

May the One Who brings harmony into the spheres on high bring peace to earth for all humanity.

Group

יְיָ עֹז לְעַמּוֹ יִתֵּן, יְיָ יְבָרֵךְ אֶת־עַמּוֹ בַשָּׁלוֹם:

God will give strength unto our people.
God will bless all people with peace.

(*The Seder text continues on page 67.*)

בָּרֵךְ.

הִנְנִי מוּכָן וּמְזֻמָּן לְקַיֵּם מִצְוַת עֲשֵׂה שֶׁל בִּרְכַּת הַמָּזוֹן. שֶׁנֶּאֱמַר: וְאָכַלְתָּ וְשָׂבָעְתָּ וּבֵרַכְתָּ אֶת־יְיָ אֱלֹהֶיךָ, עַל־הָאָרֶץ הַטּוֹבָה אֲשֶׁר נָתַן־לָךְ: לְשֵׁם יִחוּד קוּדְשָׁא בְּרִיךְ־הוּא וּשְׁכִינְתֵּיהּ בְּשֵׁם כָּל־יִשְׂרָאֵל.

הַמְזַמֵּן אוֹמֵר: רַבּוֹתַי נְבָרֵךְ.

הַמְסֻבִּים עוֹנִים: יְהִי שֵׁם יְיָ מְבֹרָךְ מֵעַתָּה וְעַד עוֹלָם.
הַמְזַמֵּן: בִּרְשׁוּת מָרָנָן וְרַבּוֹתַי, נְבָרֵךְ אֱלֹהֵינוּ שֶׁאָכַלְנוּ מִשֶּׁלּוֹ.
הַמְסֻבִּים: בָּרוּךְ אֱלֹהֵינוּ שֶׁאָכַלְנוּ מִשֶּׁלּוֹ וּבְטוּבוֹ חָיִינוּ.
הַמְזַמֵּן: בָּרוּךְ אֱלֹהֵינוּ שֶׁאָכַלְנוּ מִשֶּׁלּוֹ וּבְטוּבוֹ חָיִינוּ.

בָּרוּךְ הוּא וּבָרוּךְ שְׁמוֹ.

בָּרוּךְ אַתָּה יְיָ אֱלֹהֵינוּ מֶלֶךְ הָעוֹלָם הַזָּן אֶת הָעוֹלָם כֻּלּוֹ בְּטוּבוֹ בְּחֵן בְּחֶסֶד וּבְרַחֲמִים הוּא נוֹתֵן לֶחֶם לְכָל־בָּשָׂר כִּי לְעוֹלָם חַסְדּוֹ: וּבְטוּבוֹ הַגָּדוֹל תָּמִיד לֹא חָסַר לָנוּ וְאַל יֶחְסַר לָנוּ מָזוֹן לְעוֹלָם וָעֶד: בַּעֲבוּר שְׁמוֹ הַגָּדוֹל כִּי הוּא אֵל זָן וּמְפַרְנֵס לַכֹּל וּמֵטִיב לַכֹּל וּמֵכִין מָזוֹן לְכָל בְּרִיּוֹתָיו אֲשֶׁר בָּרָא. בָּרוּךְ אַתָּה יְיָ הַזָּן אֶת־הַכֹּל:

נוֹדֶה לְּךָ יְיָ אֱלֹהֵינוּ עַל שֶׁהִנְחַלְתָּ לַאֲבוֹתֵינוּ אֶרֶץ חֶמְדָּה טוֹבָה וּרְחָבָה וְעַל

שֶׁהוֹצֵאתָנוּ יְיָ אֱלֹהֵינוּ מֵאֶרֶץ מִצְרַיִם וּפְדִיתָנוּ מִבֵּית עֲבָדִים וְעַל בְּרִיתְךָ שֶׁחָתַמְתָּ בִּבְשָׂרֵנוּ וְעַל תּוֹרָתְךָ שֶׁלִּמַּדְתָּנוּ וְעַל חֻקֶּיךָ שֶׁהוֹדַעְתָּנוּ וְעַל חַיִּים חֵן וָחֶסֶד שֶׁחוֹנַנְתָּנוּ וְעַל אֲכִילַת מָזוֹן שָׁאַתָּה זָן וּמְפַרְנֵס אוֹתָנוּ תָּמִיד בְּכָל יוֹם וּבְכָל עֵת וּבְכָל שָׁעָה:

וְעַל הַכֹּל יְיָ אֱלֹהֵינוּ אֲנַחְנוּ מוֹדִים לָךְ וּמְבָרְכִים אוֹתָךְ יִתְבָּרַךְ שִׁמְךָ בְּפִי כָּל חַי תָּמִיד לְעוֹלָם וָעֶד: כַּכָּתוּב וְאָכַלְתָּ וְשָׂבָעְתָּ וּבֵרַכְתָּ אֶת־יְיָ אֱלֹהֶיךָ עַל הָאָרֶץ הַטֹּבָה אֲשֶׁר נָתַן לָךְ. בָּרוּךְ אַתָּה יְיָ עַל הָאָרֶץ וְעַל הַמָּזוֹן:

רַחֶם־נָא יְיָ אֱלֹהֵינוּ עַל יִשְׂרָאֵל עַמֶּךָ וְעַל יְרוּשָׁלַיִם עִירֶךָ וְעַל צִיּוֹן מִשְׁכַּן כְּבוֹדֶךָ וְעַל מַלְכוּת בֵּית דָּוִד מְשִׁיחֶךָ. וְעַל הַבַּיִת הַגָּדוֹל וְהַקָּדוֹשׁ שֶׁנִּקְרָא שִׁמְךָ עָלָיו. אֱלֹהֵינוּ אָבִינוּ רְעֵנוּ זוּנֵנוּ פַּרְנְסֵנוּ וְכַלְכְּלֵנוּ וְהַרְוִיחֵנוּ וְהַרְוַח לָנוּ יְיָ אֱלֹהֵינוּ מְהֵרָה מִכָּל־צָרוֹתֵינוּ וְנָא אַל־תַּצְרִיכֵנוּ יְיָ אֱלֹהֵינוּ לֹא לִידֵי מַתְּנַת בָּשָׂר וָדָם וְלֹא לִידֵי הַלְוָאָתָם. כִּי אִם לְיָדְךָ הַמְּלֵאָה הַפְּתוּחָה הַקְּדוֹשָׁה וְהָרְחָבָה שֶׁלֹּא נֵבוֹשׁ וְלֹא נִכָּלֵם לְעוֹלָם וָעֶד:

(On Sabbath continue here:)

רְצֵה וְהַחֲלִיצֵנוּ יְיָ אֱלֹהֵינוּ בְּמִצְוֹתֶיךָ וּבְמִצְוַת יוֹם הַשְּׁבִיעִי. הַשַּׁבָּת הַגָּדוֹל וְהַקָּדוֹשׁ הַזֶּה. כִּי יוֹם זֶה גָּדוֹל וְקָדוֹשׁ הוּא לְפָנֶיךָ לִשְׁבָּת בּוֹ וְלָנוּחַ בּוֹ בְּאַהֲבָה כְּמִצְוַת רְצוֹנֶךָ: וּבִרְצוֹנְךָ הָנִיחַ לָנוּ יְיָ אֱלֹהֵינוּ שֶׁלֹּא תְהֵא צָרָה וְיָגוֹן וַאֲנָחָה בְּיוֹם מְנוּחָתֵנוּ. וְהַרְאֵנוּ יְיָ אֱלֹהֵינוּ בְּנֶחָמַת צִיּוֹן עִירֶךָ וּבְבִנְיַן יְרוּשָׁלַיִם עִיר קָדְשֶׁךָ. כִּי אַתָּה הוּא בַּעַל הַיְשׁוּעוֹת וּבַעַל הַנֶּחָמוֹת:

(On weekdays continue here:)

אֱלֹהֵינוּ וֵאלֹהֵי אֲבוֹתֵינוּ, יַעֲלֶה וְיָבֹא, וְיַגִּיעַ, וְיֵרָאֶה, וְיֵרָצֶה וְיִשָּׁמַע וְיִפָּקֵד וְיִזָּכֵר זִכְרוֹנֵנוּ וּפִקְדוֹנֵנוּ וְזִכְרוֹן אֲבוֹתֵינוּ. וְזִכְרוֹן מָשִׁיחַ בֶּן דָּוִד עַבְדֶּךָ: וְזִכְרוֹן יְרוּשָׁלַיִם עִיר קָדְשֶׁךָ. וְזִכְרוֹן כָּל עַמְּךָ בֵּית יִשְׂרָאֵל לְפָנֶיךָ. לִפְלֵטָה לְטוֹבָה לְחֵן וּלְחֶסֶד וּלְרַחֲמִים לְחַיִּים וּלְשָׁלוֹם בְּיוֹם חַג הַמַּצּוֹת הַזֶּה. זָכְרֵנוּ יְיָ אֱלֹהֵינוּ בּוֹ לְטוֹבָה וּפָקְדֵנוּ בוֹ לִבְרָכָה. וְהוֹשִׁיעֵנוּ בוֹ לְחַיִּים טוֹבִים. וּבִדְבַר יְשׁוּעָה וְרַחֲמִים חוּס וְחָנֵּנוּ. וְרַחֵם עָלֵינוּ וְהוֹשִׁיעֵנוּ כִּי אֵלֶיךָ עֵינֵינוּ. כִּי אֵל מֶלֶךְ חַנּוּן וְרַחוּם אָתָּה:

וּבְנֵה יְרוּשָׁלַיִם עִיר הַקֹּדֶשׁ בִּמְהֵרָה בְיָמֵינוּ: בָּרוּךְ אַתָּה יְיָ, בּוֹנֵה בְרַחֲמָיו יְרוּשָׁלָיִם. אָמֵן:

בָּרוּךְ אַתָּה יְיָ, אֱלֹהֵינוּ מֶלֶךְ הָעוֹלָם, הָאֵל אָבִינוּ, מַלְכֵּנוּ, אַדִּירֵנוּ, בּוֹרְאֵנוּ, גּוֹאֲלֵנוּ, יוֹצְרֵנוּ קְדוֹשֵׁנוּ, קְדוֹשׁ יַעֲקֹב. רוֹעֵנוּ רוֹעֵה יִשְׂרָאֵל. הַמֶּלֶךְ הַטּוֹב, וְהַמֵּטִיב לַכֹּל, שֶׁבְּכָל־יוֹם וָיוֹם הוּא הֵטִיב, הוּא מֵטִיב, הוּא יֵיטִיב לָנוּ: הוּא גְמָלָנוּ. הוּא גוֹמְלֵנוּ. הוּא יִגְמְלֵנוּ לָעַד. לְחֵן וּלְחֶסֶד, וּלְרַחֲמִים וּלְרֶוַח. הַצָּלָה וְהַצְלָחָה, בְּרָכָה וִישׁוּעָה. נֶחָמָה, פַּרְנָסָה וְכַלְכָּלָה. וְרַחֲמִים, וְחַיִּים וְשָׁלוֹם, וְכָל־טוֹב, וּמִכָּל־טוּב לְעוֹלָם אַל־יְחַסְּרֵנוּ: הָרַחֲמָן, הוּא יִמְלוֹךְ עָלֵינוּ לְעוֹלָם וָעֶד: הָרַחֲמָן, הוּא יִתְבָּרַךְ בַּשָּׁמַיִם וּבָאָרֶץ: הָרַחֲמָן הוּא יִשְׁתַּבַּח לְדוֹר דּוֹרִים,

וְיִתְפָּאַר בָּנוּ לָעַד וּלְנֶצַח נְצָחִים וְיִתְהַדַּר בָּנוּ לָעַד וּלְעוֹלְמֵי עוֹלָמִים: הָרַחֲמָן, הוּא יְפַרְנְסֵנוּ בְּכָבוֹד: הָרַחֲמָן הוּא יִשְׁבּוֹר עֻלֵּנוּ מֵעַל צַוָּארֵנוּ, וְהוּא יוֹלִיכֵנוּ קוֹמְמִיּוּת לְאַרְצֵנוּ: הָרַחֲמָן, הוּא יִשְׁלַח לָנוּ, בְּרָכָה מְרֻבָּה בַּבַּיִת הַזֶּה: וְעַל שֻׁלְחָן זֶה שֶׁאָכַלְנוּ עָלָיו: הָרַחֲמָן הוּא יִשְׁלַח לָנוּ אֶת־אֵלִיָּהוּ הַנָּבִיא זָכוּר לַטּוֹב, וִיבַשֶּׂר־לָנוּ בְּשׂוֹרוֹת טוֹבוֹת יְשׁוּעוֹת וְנֶחָמוֹת: הָרַחֲמָן הוּא יְבָרֵךְ (אִם יֵשׁ לוֹ אָב וְאִם יֹאמַר) אֶת־אָבִי מוֹרִי בַּעַל הַבַּיִת הַזֶּה, וְאֶת־אִמִּי מוֹרָתִי, בַּעֲלַת הַבַּיִת הַזֶּה. אוֹתָם וְאֶת־בֵּיתָם, וְאֶת־זַרְעָם וְאֶת־כָּל־אֲשֶׁר לָהֶם. (וְאִם הוּא נָשׂוּי יֹאמַר) אוֹתִי וְאֶת אִשְׁתִּי וְאֶת זַרְעִי וְכָל הַמְסֻבִּים כָּאן אוֹתָנוּ וְאֶת־כָּל־אֲשֶׁר לָנוּ, כְּמוֹ שֶׁנִּתְבָּרְכוּ אֲבוֹתֵינוּ אַבְרָהָם יִצְחָק וְיַעֲקֹב. בַּכֹּל מִכֹּל כֹּל. כֵּן יְבָרֵךְ אוֹתָנוּ, כֻּלָּנוּ יַחַד, בִּבְרָכָה שְׁלֵמָה. וְנֹאמַר אָמֵן:

בַּמָּרוֹם יְלַמְּדוּ עֲלֵיהֶם וְעָלֵינוּ זְכוּת, שֶׁתְּהֵא לְמִשְׁמֶרֶת שָׁלוֹם: וְנִשָּׂא בְרָכָה מֵאֵת יְיָ, וּצְדָקָה מֵאֱלֹהֵי יִשְׁעֵנוּ. וְנִמְצָא חֵן וְשֵׂכֶל טוֹב בְּעֵינֵי אֱלֹהִים וְאָדָם:

(On Sabbath this line is added:)

הָרַחֲמָן הוּא יַנְחִילֵנוּ יוֹם שֶׁכֻּלּוֹ שַׁבָּת וּמְנוּחָה לְחַיֵּי הָעוֹלָמִים:

הָרַחֲמָן, הוּא יַנְחִילֵנוּ יוֹם שֶׁכֻּלּוֹ טוֹב.

הָרַחֲמָן, הוּא יְזַכֵּנוּ לִימוֹת הַמָּשִׁיחַ וּלְחַיֵּי הָעוֹלָם הַבָּא.

מִגְדוֹל יְשׁוּעוֹת מַלְכּוֹ, וְעֹשֶׂה חֶסֶד לִמְשִׁיחוֹ, לְדָוִד וּלְזַרְעוֹ עַד עוֹלָם. עֹשֶׂה שָׁלוֹם בִּמְרוֹמָיו, הוּא יַעֲשֶׂה שָׁלוֹם עָלֵינוּ וְעַל כָּל יִשְׂרָאֵל, וְאִמְרוּ אָמֵן:

יְראוּ אֶת־יְיָ קְדֹשָׁיו, כִּי אֵין מַחְסוֹר לִירֵאָיו: כְּפִירִים רָשׁוּ וְרָעֵבוּ וְדֹרְשֵׁי יְיָ לֹא־יַחְסְרוּ כָל־טוֹב: הוֹדוּ לַייָ כִּי טוֹב כִּי לְעוֹלָם חַסְדּוֹ: פּוֹתֵחַ אֶת־יָדֶךָ, וּמַשְׂבִּיעַ לְכָל־חַי רָצוֹן: בָּרוּךְ הַגֶּבֶר אֲשֶׁר יִבְטַח בַּייָ, וְהָיָה יְיָ מִבְטַחוֹ: נַעַר הָיִיתִי גַּם זָקַנְתִּי וְלֹא רָאִיתִי צַדִּיק נֶעֱזָב וְזַרְעוֹ מְבַקֶּשׁ־לָחֶם: יְיָ עֹז לְעַמּוֹ יִתֵּן, יְיָ יְבָרֵךְ אֶת־עַמּוֹ בַשָּׁלוֹם:

* * *

כּוֹס בְּרָכָה

Kos B'raḥa, the Third Cup—the Cup of Blessing

Leader

Together we take up the cup of wine, now recalling the third divine promise:

שֶׁנֶּאֱמַר וְגָאַלְתִּי אֶתְכֶם בִּזְרוֹעַ נְטוּיָה:

Group

Exodus 6:6

As it is written: "*I will redeem you* with an outstretched arm."

בָּרוּךְ אַתָּה יְיָ אֱלֹהֵינוּ מֶלֶךְ הָעוֹלָם בּוֹרֵא פְּרִי הַגָּפֶן:

Baruḥ Atah Adonai Eloheinu Meleḥ ha-olam borei p'ri ha-gafen.
We praise Thee, our God, Sovereign of the universe, Who has created the fruit of the vine.

(*All drink the third cup of wine.*)

כּוֹס אֵלִיָּהוּ

Kos Eliyahu, the Cup of Elijah

(*Elijah, the prophet from the village of Tishbi in Gilead, challenged the injustice of the king and overthrew the worship of Baal. He healed the humble sick and helped the widowed. As to the end of his days on earth, his disciple Elisha had a vision of Elijah being carried to the skies in a chariot of fire. Legend has it that Elijah returns to earth, from time to time, to befriend the helpless.*

This man of mystery became associated with the End of Days, with the Messianic hopes of our people. The prophet Malachi promised that Elijah would come to turn the hearts of parents to children, and the hearts of children to parents, and to announce the coming of the Messiah when all mankind would celebrate freedom.
Hence, he has a place in every Seder. We open the door that he may enter, and set a cup of wine to represent the final Messianic promise for us and for all peoples: "I will bring you into the Land.")

Leader

How many images this moment brings to mind,
how many thoughts
the memory of Elijah stirs in us!
The times when we were objects of distrust,
when our doors were open to surveillance,
when ignorant and hostile men
forced our doors with terror!

Group

כִּי־אָכַל אֶת־יַעֲקֹב וְאֶת־נָוֵהוּ הֵשַׁמּוּ:

They devoured Jacob, laid waste his habitation. *Psalm 79:7*

Leader

The injustice of this world still brings to mind Elijah who in defense of justice, challenged power. In many tales from Jewish lore, he reappears to help the weak. Our people always prayed:

How many images . . .
the memory of Elijah stirs in us.

Group

הָרַחֲמָן. הוּא יִשְׁלַח לָנוּ אֶת־אֵלִיָּהוּ הַנָּבִיא זָכוּר לַטּוֹב וִיבַשֶּׂר־לָנוּ בְּשׂוֹרוֹת טוֹבוֹת יְשׁוּעוֹת וְנֶחָמוֹת:

May the All Merciful send us Elijah the Prophet to comfort us with tidings of deliverance. *The Siddur*

Leader

For every undecided question, then, of pain and sorrow, of unrewarded worth and unrequited evil, Elijah would someday provide the answer.

Group

תִּשְׁבִּי יְתָרֵץ קוּשְׁיוֹת וּבְעָיוֹת.

There are links between heaven and earth which promise an answer and resolution to life's perplexities.

Leader

Elijah opens up for us the realm of mystery and wonder.

Let us now open the door for Elijah!

(A child or children are sent to open a door to the outside. As the door is opened:)

Group

הִנֵּה אָנֹכִי שֹׁלֵחַ לָכֶם אֵת אֵלִיָּה הַנָּבִיא לִפְנֵי בּוֹא יוֹם יְהוָה הַגָּדוֹל וְהַנּוֹרָא: וְהֵשִׁיב לֵב־אָבוֹת עַל־בָּנִים וְלֵב בָּנִים עַל־אֲבוֹתָם פֶּן־אָבוֹא וְהִכֵּיתִי אֶת־הָאָרֶץ חֵרֶם:

Behold, I will send you Elijah the prophet, and he will turn the hearts of the parents to the children and the hearts of the children to the parents before the coming of the great and awesome Day of God! *Malachi 3:23–24*

Leader

FROM BEYOND, ELIJAH'S SPIRIT ENTERS IN THESE WALLS
AND TASTES AGAIN WITH US THE WINE OF ENDLESS PROMISE:

Group

וְהֵבֵאתִי אֶתְכֶם אֶל־הָאָרֶץ אֲנִי יְהוָה:

I WILL BRING YOU INTO THE LAND . . . I, **יהוה**. *(Door is closed.)* *Exodus 6:8*

𝄞 22 (*All sing* Eliyahu Hanavi.)

אֵלִיָּהוּ הַנָּבִיא, אֵלִיָּהוּ הַתִּשְׁבִּי,
אֵלִיָּהוּ, אֵלִיָּהוּ, אֵלִיָּהוּ הַגִּלְעָדִי,
בִּמְהֵרָה בְיָמֵינוּ יָבֹא אֵלֵינוּ
עִם מָשִׁיחַ בֶּן דָּוִד, עִם מָשִׁיחַ בֶּן דָּוִד.

HALLEL, PSALMS OF PRAISE

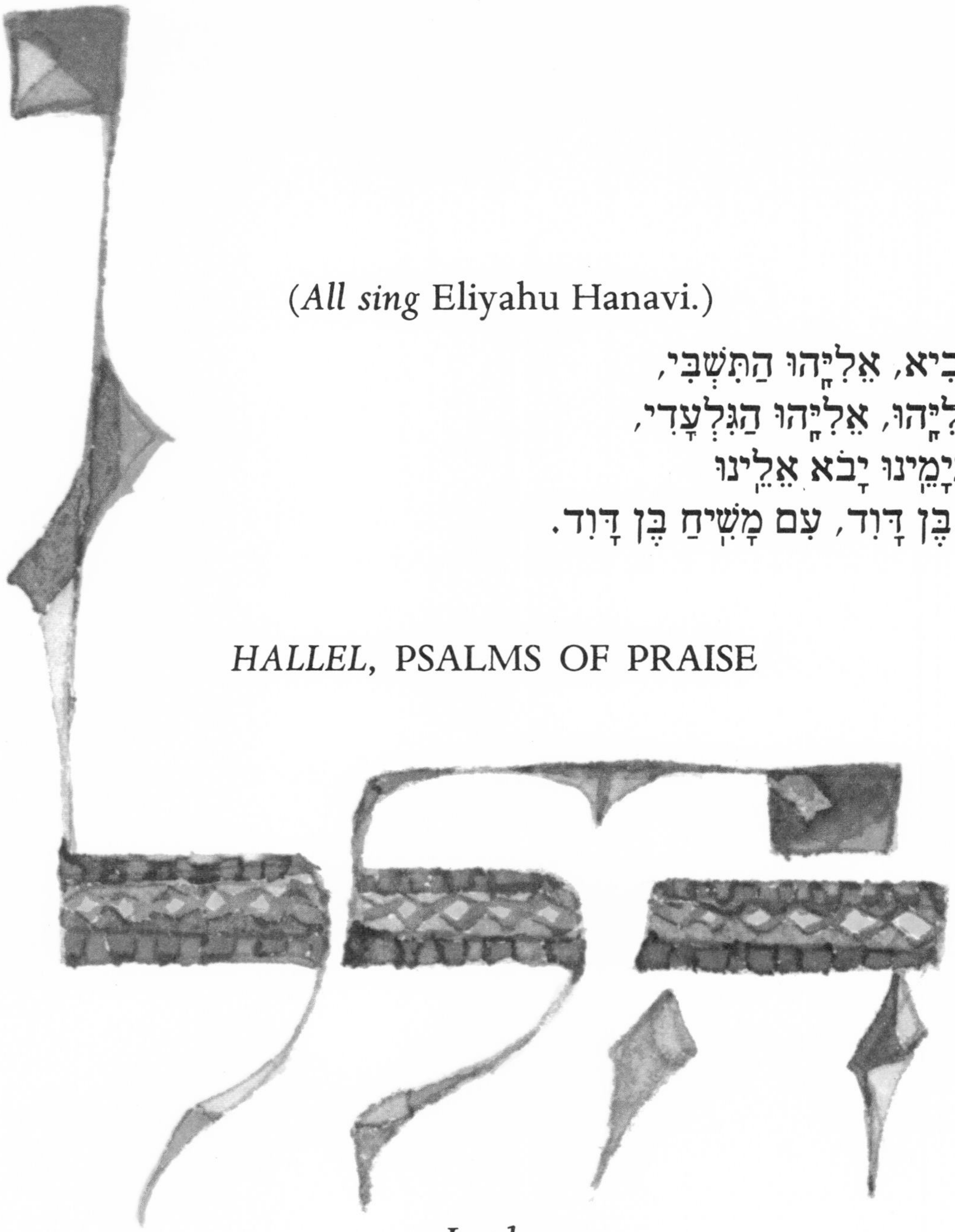

Leader

Halleluyah. We praise. Our song is one with the chants of the Levites in the days of the Temple's glory. On this very festival, they sang their psalms of praise, the Hallel.

Our song is one with all the hymns of flesh and blood which sing of the triumph of people together over the powers of destruction.

Group

And will be one with the praise songs of all peoples:
Praise, for the earth restored to its goodness;
Praise, for people restored to themselves;
Praise, for life fulfilled in sacred celebration:

(*Read or sing any of the following selections from Psalms 115 through 118.*)

𝄞 23 Praise God, all ye nations! הַלְלוּ אֶת־יְיָ כָּל־גּוֹיִם.

Sing praises, all ye peoples,
For the faithfulness of God
has been mighty with us,
And God's truth is forever.
Halleluyah.

שַׁבְּחוּהוּ כָּל־הָאֻמִּים:
כִּי גָבַר עָלֵינוּ חַסְדּוֹ
וֶאֱמֶת־יְיָ לְעוֹלָם הַלְלוּיָהּ:

*

𝄞 24

O give thanks unto God for He is good,
for His truthfulness is forever.
As Israel shall bear witness:
the truth of God is eternal.
As the House of Aaron now proclaims:
Infinite is His mercy.
As all will declare who revere His name:
Endless is His lovingkindness!

הוֹדוּ לַייָ כִּי טוֹב
כִּי לְעוֹלָם חַסְדּוֹ:
יֹאמַר־נָא יִשְׂרָאֵל
כִּי לְעוֹלָם חַסְדּוֹ:
יֹאמְרוּ־נָא בֵית אַהֲרֹן
כִּי לְעוֹלָם חַסְדּוֹ:
יֹאמְרוּ־נָא יִרְאֵי יְיָ
כִּי לְעוֹלָם חַסְדּוֹ:

𝄞 25

Open up, O gates of righteousness,
That we may enter and sing your praise!
To You, O God,
Does Israel's song arise
Wondrous in our eyes.

פִּתְחוּ־לִי שַׁעֲרֵי־צֶדֶק.
אָבֹא־בָם אוֹדֶה יָהּ:
עָזִּי וְזִמְרָת יָהּ. וַיְהִי־לִי
לִישׁוּעָה:

This is the day
Which God has ordained for us,
For we were destined of old.
We lift our voice.
Our souls within rejoice.
God's endless praise be told!

זֶה־הַיּוֹם עָשָׂה יְהוָֹה
נָגִילָה וְנִשְׂמְחָה בוֹ:

𝄞 24A

God, we beseech You, Redeem!
God, we pray You, Deliver!
God, we beseech You, Prevail!
God, we beseech You, Triumph!

אָנָּא יְיָ הוֹשִׁיעָה נָּא:
אָנָּא יְיָ הוֹשִׁיעָה נָּא:
אָנָּא יְיָ הַצְלִיחָה נָא:
אָנָּא יְיָ הַצְלִיחָה נָא:

*

Why should the nations say,
"Where now is their God?"
"Where *now* is their God?"
Their idols are silver and gold;
Their idols are gold,
The work of human hands.
Unseeing eyes they have,
And mouths, but no true speech;

לֹא לָנוּ יְיָ לֹא לָנוּ
כִּי לְשִׁמְךָ תֵּן כָּבוֹד.
עַל־חַסְדְּךָ עַל־אֲמִתֶּךָ:
לָמָּה יֹאמְרוּ הַגּוֹיִם.
אַיֵּה־נָא אֱלֹהֵיהֶם:
וֵאלֹהֵינוּ בַשָּׁמָיִם.
כֹּל אֲשֶׁר־חָפֵץ עָשָׂה:

Speedily, in our days . . .
Messiah, son of David.

דוד המלך

Hands that cannot reach nor touch;
Deaf they are to others' words;
Inert, without the vivid breath of life.
Those who make them will be as they are,
Their worshipers become like them,
Yes, all who put their trust in them!

עֲצַבֵּיהֶם כֶּסֶף וְזָהָב.
מַעֲשֵׂה יְדֵי אָדָם:
פֶּה לָהֶם וְלֹא יְדַבֵּרוּ.
עֵינַיִם לָהֶם וְלֹא יִרְאוּ:
אָזְנַיִם לָהֶם וְלֹא יִשְׁמָעוּ.
אַף לָהֶם וְלֹא יְרִיחוּן:
יְדֵיהֶם וְלֹא יְמִישׁוּן
רַגְלֵיהֶם וְלֹא יְהַלֵּכוּ.
לֹא־יֶהְגּוּ בִּגְרוֹנָם:
כְּמוֹהֶם יִהְיוּ עֹשֵׂיהֶם.
כֹּל אֲשֶׁר־בֹּטֵחַ בָּהֶם:

*

Leader כּוֹס־יְשׁוּעוֹת אֶשָּׂא. וּבְשֵׁם יְיָ אֶקְרָא:

I lift up the cup of deliverance and call upon the Name of God.

Group וַאֲנַחְנוּ נְבָרֵךְ יָהּ מֵעַתָּה וְעַד־עוֹלָם הַלְלוּיָהּ:

We will praise our God forever.

Leader מִן־הַמֵּצַר קָרָאתִי יָהּ. עָנָנִי בַמֶּרְחָב יָהּ:

Out of the depths, I called upon God!
Who answered me with great deliverance.

Group לֹא־אָמוּת כִּי־אֶחְיֶה. וַאֲסַפֵּר מַעֲשֵׂה־יָהּ:

We will not die, but live.

Leader לֹא־הַמֵּתִים יְהַלְלוּ־יָהּ. וְלֹא כָּל־יֹרְדֵי דוּמָה:

The dead praise not יהוה, nor any that go down into silence.

Group וַאֲנַחְנוּ נְבָרֵךְ יָהּ מֵעַתָּה וְעַד־עוֹלָם הַלְלוּיָהּ:

But we will praise יהוה forever.

Leader אֶתְהַלֵּךְ לִפְנֵי יְיָ. בְּאַרְצוֹת הַחַיִּים:

I shall walk before the Lord in the land of the living.

Group לֹא־אָמוּת כִּי־אֶחְיֶה. וַאֲסַפֵּר מַעֲשֵׂה־יָהּ:

We will not die, but live.

Leader עָזִּי וְזִמְרָת יָהּ. וַיְהִי־לִי לִישׁוּעָה:

God is my strength and my song, and God has become my triumph.

וַאֲנַחְנוּ נְבָרֵךְ יָהּ מֵעַתָּה וְעַד־עוֹלָם הַלְלוּיָהּ׃

Group

And we will praise our God forever.

אֶבֶן מָאֲסוּ הַבּוֹנִים. הָיְתָה לְרֹאשׁ פִּנָּה׃

Leader

The stone which the builders rejected
Has become the chief cornerstone.

לֹא־אָמוּת כִּי־אֶחְיֶה. וַאֲסַפֵּר מַעֲשֵׂה־יָהּ׃
וַאֲנַחְנוּ נְבָרֵךְ יָהּ מֵעַתָּה וְעַד־עוֹלָם הַלְלוּיָהּ׃

Group

We will not die, but live,
Live to declare the works of God,
And we will praise **יהוה** forever.

נִשְׁמַת

נִשְׁמַת כָּל־חַי תְּבָרֵךְ אֶת־שִׁמְךָ יְיָ אֱלֹהֵינוּ. וְרוּחַ כָּל־בָּשָׂר תְּפָאֵר וּתְרוֹמֵם זִכְרְךָ מַלְכֵּנוּ תָּמִיד. מִן־הָעוֹלָם וְעַד־הָעוֹלָם אַתָּה אֵל וּמִבַּלְעָדֶיךָ אֵין לָנוּ מֶלֶךְ גּוֹאֵל וּמוֹשִׁיעַ פּוֹדֶה וּמַצִּיל וּמְפַרְנֵס וּמְרַחֵם בְּכָל־עֵת צָרָה וְצוּקָה אֵין־לָנוּ מֶלֶךְ אֶלָּא אָתָּה׃ אֱלֹהֵי הָרִאשׁוֹנִים וְהָאַחֲרוֹנִים. אֱלוֹהַּ כָּל־בְּרִיּוֹת אֲדוֹן כָּל־תּוֹלָדוֹת. הַמְהֻלָּל בְּרֹב הַתִּשְׁבָּחוֹת. הַמְנַהֵג עוֹלָמוֹ בְּחֶסֶד וּבְרִיּוֹתָיו בְּרַחֲמִים. וַיְיָ לֹא־יָנוּם וְלֹא־יִישָׁן׃ הַמְעוֹרֵר יְשֵׁנִים וְהַמֵּקִיץ נִרְדָּמִים וְהַמֵּשִׂיחַ אִלְּמִים וְהַמַּתִּיר אֲסוּרִים וְהַסּוֹמֵךְ נוֹפְלִים וְהַזּוֹקֵף כְּפוּפִים. לְךָ לְבַדְּךָ אֲנַחְנוּ מוֹדִים׃ אִלּוּ פִינוּ מָלֵא שִׁירָה כַּיָּם וּלְשׁוֹנֵנוּ רִנָּה כַּהֲמוֹן גַּלָּיו וְשִׂפְתוֹתֵינוּ שֶׁבַח כְּמֶרְחֲבֵי רָקִיעַ וְעֵינֵינוּ מְאִירוֹת כַּשֶּׁמֶשׁ וְכַיָּרֵחַ וְיָדֵינוּ פְרוּשׂוֹת כְּנִשְׁרֵי שָׁמָיִם וְרַגְלֵינוּ קַלּוֹת כָּאַיָּלוֹת. אֵין אֲנַחְנוּ מַסְפִּיקִים לְהוֹדוֹת לְךָ יְיָ אֱלֹהֵינוּ וֵאלֹהֵי אֲבוֹתֵינוּ וּלְבָרֵךְ אֶת־שְׁמֶךָ עַל־אַחַת מֵאָלֶף אֶלֶף אַלְפֵי אֲלָפִים וְרִבֵּי רְבָבוֹת פְּעָמִים הַטּוֹבוֹת שֶׁעָשִׂיתָ עִם־אֲבוֹתֵינוּ וְעִמָּנוּ׃ מִמִּצְרַיִם גְּאַלְתָּנוּ יְיָ אֱלֹהֵינוּ וּמִבֵּית עֲבָדִים פְּדִיתָנוּ. בְּרָעָב זַנְתָּנוּ וּבְשָׂבָע כִּלְכַּלְתָּנוּ. מֵחֶרֶב הִצַּלְתָּנוּ וּמִדֶּבֶר מִלַּטְתָּנוּ. וּמֵחֳלָיִם רָעִים וְנֶאֱמָנִים דִּלִּיתָנוּ׃ עַד־הֵנָּה עֲזָרוּנוּ רַחֲמֶיךָ. וְלֹא־עֲזָבוּנוּ חֲסָדֶיךָ. וְאַל־תִּטְּשֵׁנוּ יְיָ אֱלֹהֵינוּ לָנֶצַח׃ עַל־כֵּן אֵבָרִים שֶׁפִּלַּגְתָּ בָּנוּ וְרוּחַ וּנְשָׁמָה שֶׁנָּפַחְתָּ בְּאַפֵּינוּ וְלָשׁוֹן אֲשֶׁר שַׂמְתָּ בְּפִינוּ. הֵן הֵם יוֹדוּ וִיבָרְכוּ וִישַׁבְּחוּ וִיפָאֲרוּ וִירוֹמְמוּ וְיַעֲרִיצוּ וְיַקְדִּישׁוּ וְיַמְלִיכוּ אֶת־שִׁמְךָ מַלְכֵּנוּ׃ כִּי כָל־פֶּה לְךָ יוֹדֶה. וְכָל־לָשׁוֹן לְךָ תִשָּׁבַע. וְכָל־בֶּרֶךְ לְךָ תִכְרַע. וְכָל־קוֹמָה לְפָנֶיךָ תִשְׁתַּחֲוֶה. וְכָל־לְבָבוֹת יִירָאוּךָ. וְכָל־קֶרֶב וּכְלָיוֹת יְזַמְּרוּ לִשְׁמֶךָ. כַּדָּבָר שֶׁכָּתוּב. כָּל־עַצְמוֹתַי תֹּאמַרְנָה יְיָ מִי כָמוֹךָ. מַצִּיל עָנִי מֵחָזָק מִמֶּנּוּ וְעָנִי וְאֶבְיוֹן מִגּוֹזְלוֹ׃ מִי יִדְמֶה־לָּךְ וּמִי יִשְׁוֶה־לָּךְ וּמִי יַעֲרָךְ־לָךְ. הָאֵל הַגָּדוֹל הַגִּבּוֹר וְהַנּוֹרָא אֵל עֶלְיוֹן קֹנֵה שָׁמַיִם וָאָרֶץ׃ נְהַלֶּלְךָ וּנְשַׁבֵּחֲךָ וּנְפָאֶרְךָ וּנְבָרֵךְ אֶת־שֵׁם קָדְשֶׁךָ. כָּאָמוּר לְדָוִד בָּרְכִי נַפְשִׁי אֶת־יְיָ וְכָל־קְרָבַי אֶת־שֵׁם קָדְשׁוֹ׃

זינג

Leader

The breath of all the living is praise of Thee, O God.
The spirit of all flesh is Thine eternal glory, O our King.
From everlasting to everlasting Thou art God.
And besides Thee, we have no sovereign, no redeemer.

Were our mouths as full of song as the sea
And our tongues with melody as the multitude of its waves,
Our eyes shining like the sun and the moon,
Our arms like soaring eagles' pinions,
Our limbs like those of the swift gazelle,
Still our power would be nought to show
The thousand myriad bounties You have bestowed
Upon our parents and on us.

But, O God, limbs and tongue and heart and mind,
Join now to praise Thy Name,
As every tongue will yet avow Thee
And every soul give Thee allegiance.

Psalm 35:10 As it is written: All my bones shall shout in joy:
O God, who is like Thee?
And as David sang:
Psalm 103:1 Praise the Lord, my whole being!
All that is within me:
Praise **יהוה**, my whole being!

(*The Seder text continues on page 79.*)

An Additional Cup Set Aside for the Future — כּוֹס יַיִן מְשֻׁמָּר לֶעָתִיד לָבוֹא

(It is, of course, the events of our time that have evoked this new experience and ritual. But the inclusion of a "fifth cup" as a meritorious mitzvah *was already discussed by the early rabbis and even praised by notable scholars—Alfasi, Rashi, Maimonides, and others. In his Haggadah, the Maharal of Prague details in full "an order of the fifth cup." As in the past, the additional "Cup of Redemption" is placed in proximity to the Hallel.*
Within this service may be found texts representative of the entire sweep of our history and tradition, texts from prophetic, rabbinic, and modern sources, including the Declaration of Independence of the State of Israel.)

(A cup is poured and held up by the leader.)

Leader — הַמַּנְחֶה:

It is still dark as we pour this cup; — חֹשֶׁךְ, עוֹד חֹשֶׁךְ וְנִשָּׂא אֶת הַכּוֹס;
But light dawns over Zion as we raise this cup, — אוּלָם עַל צִיּוֹן אוֹר שַׁחַר זוֹרֵחַ;
For the day when we will tell — עַד יוֹם תְּסֻפַּר

Our arms
like soaring eagles' pinions . . .

Of the Deliverance of all.
We set aside this cup
As a sign of hope,
For the beginning of Redemption.

עַל פְּדוּת הַבְּרִיאָה
נְשַׁמֵּר אֶת הַכּוֹס,
כּוֹס אוֹת לְחָזוֹן, לְתִקְוָה—הַגְשָׁמָה,
כּוֹס אוֹת לְאַתְחַלְתָּא דִגְאֻלָּה.

Group

הַקָּהָל:

As a sign of the beginning of Redemption,
The people Israel lives!

לְאוֹת אַתְחַלְתָּא דִגְאֻלָּה,
עַם יִשְׂרָאֵל חַי!

Leader

הַמַּנְחֶה:

Passing through waters
amidst signs and wonders
was this our people born!
Out of the fiery furnace,
seared in body and soul,
reborn in self-redemption,
Finding favor in the wilderness.

תּוֹךְ הַמַּיִם עָבַר עַם זוֹ, עַמֵּנוּ.
קֶרֶב אוֹתוֹת וּמוֹפְתִים נוֹלַד;
וּמִגּוֹא אַתּוּן נוּרָא יָקְדְתָּא
יָצָא, בְּגוּף וּבְנֶפֶשׁ נִצְרָב;
קָם לִתְחִיָּה, לְחַדֵּשׁ חַיָּיו;
עַם שְׂרִידֵי חֶרֶב עָטָה חֵן,
מָצָא עוֹז וּמִשְׁכָּן בְּמִדְבַּר נְעוּרָיו.

Group

הַקָּהָל:

The people Israel lives!
This people which You have formed
Still lives—to tell of Your glory.
The people of Israel lives!

עַם יִשְׂרָאֵל חַי,
עַם זוּ יָצַרְתָּ לָךְ
עוֹד חַי, וּתְהִלָּתְךָ יְסַפֵּרוּ.
עַם יִשְׂרָאֵל חַי!

Leader

הַמַּנְחֶה:

Through the great struggle,
Toward the fulfillment
Of our longing
For the redemption of Israel,

בְּמַעֲרָכָה הַגְּדוֹלָה
עַל הַגְשָׁמַת שְׁאִיפַת דּוֹרוֹת
לִגְאֻלַּת יִשְׂרָאֵל,

Group

הַקָּהָל:

We and our children will live,
The people of Israel will live.

אָנוּ וּבָנֵינוּ נִחְיֶה!
עַם יִשְׂרָאֵל יִחְיֶה!

Leader

המַּנְחֶה:

From the holy mountain we see anew
The mystery and glory of our past.
In the new light which rises over Zion,
And throughout all our habitations,
Before us still we dimly glimpse
our greatest tasks, our finest work,
our most worthy hours:

מֵהַר הַקֹּדֶשׁ שׁוּב נִרְאֶה
אֶת הוֹד פֶּלֶא תּוֹלְדוֹת עַמֵּנוּ.
וּבְאוֹר חָדָשׁ עַל צִיּוֹן מֵאִיר
תּוֹךְ אֲפְלוּלִית, שׁוּב נִרְאֶה בֶּעָתִיד
עוֹד לָבוֹא
–גֹּדֶל תַּפְקִידֵנוּ
–שֶׁבַח עֲבוֹדָתֵנוּ
–דְּמִי יָמֵינוּ!

Group

הַקָּהָל:

To plant, to build, and to bless,
Wherever the people of Israel lives!

לִבְנוֹת וְלִנְטוֹעַ, וּלְבָרֵךְ,
כָּל מָקוֹם בַּאֲשֶׁר עַם יִשְׂרָאֵל חַי!

בָּרוּךְ אַתָּה יְיָ אֱלֹהֵינוּ מֶלֶךְ הָעוֹלָם אֲשֶׁר קִדְּשָׁנוּ בְּמִצְוֹתָיו וְצִוָּנוּ לְחַדֵּשׁ אֶת תִּקְוַת הַגְּאוּלָּה:

We praise Thee, O God, Sovereign of Existence,
Who has sanctified us with Thy commandment
And commanded us to renew the hope of Redemption!

(*The cup is set down untasted.*)

𝄞 26 Am Yisra–eil chai,
Ad beli dai,
Od avinu chai!

עַם יִשְׂרָאֵל חַי,
עַד בְּלִי דַי,
עוֹד אָבִינוּ חַי!

* * *

Leader

With merriment and song and poem we celebrate the Feast of Freedom.

אֶחָד מִי יוֹדֵעַ?

Who Knows One?

𝄞 27,14 אֶחָד מִי יוֹדֵעַ, אֶחָד אֲנִי יוֹדֵעַ:
אֶחָד אֱלֹהֵינוּ שֶׁבַּשָּׁמַיִם וּבָאָרֶץ.

שְׁנַיִם מִי יוֹדֵעַ, שְׁנַיִם אֲנִי יוֹדֵעַ:
שְׁנֵי לֻחוֹת הַבְּרִית,
אֶחָד אֱלֹהֵינוּ שֶׁבַּשָּׁמַיִם וּבָאָרֶץ.

שְׁלֹשָׁה מִי יוֹדֵעַ, שְׁלֹשָׁה אֲנִי יוֹדֵעַ:
שְׁלֹשָׁה אָבוֹת, שְׁנֵי לֻחוֹת הַבְּרִית,
אֶחָד אֱלֹהֵינוּ שֶׁבַּשָּׁמַיִם וּבָאָרֶץ.

אַרְבַּע מִי יוֹדֵעַ, אַרְבַּע אֲנִי יוֹדֵעַ:
אַרְבַּע אִמָּהוֹת, שְׁלֹשָׁה אָבוֹת, שְׁנֵי לֻחוֹת הַבְּרִית,
אֶחָד אֱלֹהֵינוּ שֶׁבַּשָּׁמַיִם וּבָאָרֶץ.

חֲמִשָּׁה מִי יוֹדֵעַ, חֲמִשָּׁה אֲנִי יוֹדֵעַ:
חֲמִשָּׁה חֻמְשֵׁי תוֹרָה, אַרְבַּע אִמָּהוֹת,
שְׁלֹשָׁה אָבוֹת, שְׁנֵי לֻחוֹת הַבְּרִית,
אֶחָד אֱלֹהֵינוּ שֶׁבַּשָּׁמַיִם וּבָאָרֶץ.

שִׁשָּׁה מִי יוֹדֵעַ, שִׁשָּׁה אֲנִי יוֹדֵעַ:
שִׁשָּׁה סִדְרֵי מִשְׁנָה, חֲמִשָּׁה חֻמְשֵׁי תוֹרָה,
אַרְבַּע אִמָּהוֹת, שְׁלֹשָׁה אָבוֹת, שְׁנֵי לֻחוֹת הַבְּרִית,
אֶחָד אֱלֹהֵינוּ שֶׁבַּשָּׁמַיִם וּבָאָרֶץ.

שִׁבְעָה מִי יוֹדֵעַ, שִׁבְעָה אֲנִי יוֹדֵעַ:
שִׁבְעָה יְמֵי שַׁבַּתָּא, שִׁשָּׁה סִדְרֵי מִשְׁנָה,
חֲמִשָּׁה חֻמְשֵׁי תוֹרָה, אַרְבַּע אִמָּהוֹת,
שְׁלֹשָׁה אָבוֹת, שְׁנֵי לֻחוֹת הַבְּרִית,
אֶחָד אֱלֹהֵינוּ שֶׁבַּשָּׁמַיִם וּבָאָרֶץ.

שְׁמֹנָה מִי יוֹדֵעַ, שְׁמֹנָה אֲנִי יוֹדֵעַ:
שְׁמֹנָה יְמֵי מִילָה, שִׁבְעָה יְמֵי שַׁבַּתָּא,
שִׁשָּׁה סִדְרֵי מִשְׁנָה, חֲמִשָּׁה חֻמְשֵׁי תוֹרָה,
אַרְבַּע אִמָּהוֹת, שְׁלֹשָׁה אָבוֹת, שְׁנֵי לֻחוֹת הַבְּרִית,
אֶחָד אֱלֹהֵינוּ שֶׁבַּשָּׁמַיִם וּבָאָרֶץ.

תִּשְׁעָה מִי יוֹדֵעַ, תִּשְׁעָה אֲנִי יוֹדֵעַ:
תִּשְׁעָה יַרְחֵי לֵדָה, שְׁמֹנָה יְמֵי מִילָה,
שִׁבְעָה יְמֵי שַׁבַּתָּא, שִׁשָּׁה סִדְרֵי מִשְׁנָה,
חֲמִשָּׁה חֻמְשֵׁי תוֹרָה, אַרְבַּע אִמָּהוֹת,
שְׁלֹשָׁה אָבוֹת, שְׁנֵי לֻחוֹת הַבְּרִית,
אֶחָד אֱלֹהֵינוּ שֶׁבַּשָּׁמַיִם וּבָאָרֶץ.

עֲשָׂרָה מִי יוֹדֵעַ, עֲשָׂרָה אֲנִי יוֹדֵעַ:
עֲשָׂרָה דִבְּרַיָּא, תִּשְׁעָה יַרְחֵי לֵדָה,
שְׁמֹנָה יְמֵי מִילָה, שִׁבְעָה יְמֵי שַׁבַּתָּא,

שִׁשָּׁה סִדְרֵי מִשְׁנָה, חֲמִשָּׁה חֻמְשֵׁי תוֹרָה,
אַרְבַּע אִמָּהוֹת, שְׁלֹשָׁה אָבוֹת, שְׁנֵי לֻחוֹת הַבְּרִית,
אֶחָד אֱלֹהֵינוּ שֶׁבַּשָּׁמַיִם וּבָאָרֶץ.

אַחַד עָשָׂר מִי יוֹדֵעַ, אַחַד עָשָׂר אֲנִי יוֹדֵעַ:
אַחַד עָשָׂר כּוֹכְבַיָּא, עֲשָׂרָה דִבְּרַיָּא,
תִּשְׁעָה יַרְחֵי לֵדָה, שְׁמוֹנָה יְמֵי מִילָה,
שִׁבְעָה יְמֵי שַׁבַּתָּא, שִׁשָּׁה סִדְרֵי מִשְׁנָה,
חֲמִשָּׁה חֻמְשֵׁי תוֹרָה, אַרְבַּע אִמָּהוֹת,
שְׁלֹשָׁה אָבוֹת, שְׁנֵי לֻחוֹת הַבְּרִית,
אֶחָד אֱלֹהֵינוּ שֶׁבַּשָּׁמַיִם וּבָאָרֶץ.

שְׁנֵים עָשָׂר מִי יוֹדֵעַ, שְׁנֵים עָשָׂר אֲנִי יוֹדֵעַ:
שְׁנֵים עָשָׂר שִׁבְטַיָּא, אַחַד עָשָׂר כּוֹכְבַיָּא,
עֲשָׂרָה דִבְּרַיָּא, תִּשְׁעָה יַרְחֵי לֵדָה,
שְׁמוֹנָה יְמֵי מִילָה, שִׁבְעָה יְמֵי שַׁבַּתָּא,
שִׁשָּׁה סִדְרֵי מִשְׁנָה, חֲמִשָּׁה חֻמְשֵׁי תוֹרָה,
אַרְבַּע אִמָּהוֹת, שְׁלֹשָׁה אָבוֹת, שְׁנֵי לֻחוֹת הַבְּרִית,
אֶחָד אֱלֹהֵינוּ שֶׁבַּשָּׁמַיִם וּבָאָרֶץ.

שְׁלֹשָׁה עָשָׂר מִי יוֹדֵעַ, שְׁלֹשָׁה עָשָׂר אֲנִי יוֹדֵעַ:
שְׁלֹשָׁה עָשָׂר מִדַּיָּא, שְׁנֵים עָשָׂר שִׁבְטַיָּא,
אַחַד עָשָׂר כּוֹכְבַיָּא, עֲשָׂרָה דִבְּרַיָּא,
תִּשְׁעָה יַרְחֵי לֵדָה, שְׁמוֹנָה יְמֵי מִילָה,
שִׁבְעָה יְמֵי שַׁבַּתָּא, שִׁשָּׁה סִדְרֵי מִשְׁנָה,
חֲמִשָּׁה חֻמְשֵׁי תוֹרָה, אַרְבַּע אִמָּהוֹת,
שְׁלֹשָׁה אָבוֹת, שְׁנֵי לֻחוֹת הַבְּרִית,
אֶחָד אֱלֹהֵינוּ שֶׁבַּשָּׁמַיִם וּבָאָרֶץ.

Who knows one? I know one.
One is our God, in heaven and on earth.

Who knows two? I know two.
Two are the tables of the commandments;
One is our God, in heaven and on earth.

Who knows three? I know three.
Three is the number of the patriarchs;
Two are the tables of the commandments;
One is our God, in heaven and on earth.

Who knows four? I know four.
Four is the number of the matriarchs;
Three, the number of patriarchs;
Two are the tables of the commandments;
One is our God, in heaven and on earth.

Who knows five? I know five.
Five books there are in the Torah;
Four is the number of the matriarchs;
Three, the number of the patriarchs;
Two are the tables of the commandments;
One is our God, in heaven and on earth.

Who knows six? I know six.
Six sections the Mishnah has;
Five books there are in the Torah;
Four is the number of matriarchs;
Three, the number of the patriarchs;
Two are the tables of the commandments;
One is our God, in heaven and on earth.

Who knows seven? I know seven.
Seven days there are in a week;
Six sections the Mishnah has;
Five books there are in the Torah;
Four is the number of matriarchs;
Three, the number of patriarchs;
Two are the tables of the commandments;
One is our God, in heaven and on earth.

Who knows eight? I know eight.
Eight are the days to the service of the covenant;
Seven days there are in the week;
Six sections the Mishnah has;
Five books there are in the Torah;
Four is the number of the matriarchs;
Three, the number of the patriarchs;
Two are the tables of the commandments;
One is our God, in heaven and on earth.

Who knows nine? I know nine.
Nine is the number of the holidays;
Eight are the days to the service of the covenant;
Seven days there are in a week;
Six sections in the Mishnah;
Five books there are in the Torah;
Four is the number of the matriarchs;

Three, the number of the patriarchs;
Two are the tables of the commandments;
One is our God, in heaven and on earth.

Who knows ten? I know ten.
Ten commandments were given on Sinai;
Nine is the number of the holidays;
Eight are the days to the service of the covenant;
Seven days there are in a week;
Six sections the Mishnah has;
Five books there are in the Torah;
Four is the number of the matriarchs;
Three, the number of the patriarchs;
Two are the tables of the commandments;
One is our God, in heaven and on earth.

Who knows eleven? I know eleven.
Eleven were the stars in Joseph's dream;
Ten commandments were given on Sinai;
Nine is the number of the holidays;
Eight are the days to the service of the covenant;
Seven days there are in a week;
Six sections the Mishnah has;
Five books there are in the Torah;
Four is the number of matriarchs;
Three, the number of the patriarchs;
Two are the tables of the commandments;
One is our God, in heaven and on earth.

Who knows twelve? I know twelve.
Twelve are the tribes of Israel;
Eleven were the stars in Joseph's dream;
Ten commandments were given on Sinai;
Nine is the number of the holidays;
Eight are the days to the service of the covenant;
Seven days there are in a week;
Six sections the Mishnah has;
Five books there are in the Torah;
Four is the number of the matriarchs;
Three, the number of the patriarchs;
Two are the tables of the commandments;
One is our God, in heaven and on earth.

Who knows thirteen? I know thirteen.
Thirteen are the attributes of God;
Twelve are the tribes of Israel;
Eleven were the stars in Joseph's dream;

רחל
לאה
רבקה
שרה

Ten commandments were given on Sinai;
Nine is the number of the holidays;
Eight are the days to the service of the covenant;
Seven days are there in a week;
Six sections the Mishnah has;
Five books there are in the Torah;
Four is the number of the matriarchs;
Three, the number of the patriarchs;
Two are the tables of the commandments;
One is our God, in heaven and on earth.

𝄞 28 (*All sing* Adir Bimluḥa)

אַדִּיר בִּמְלוּכָה. בָּחוּר כַּהֲלָכָה.
גְּדוּדָיו יֹאמְרוּ לוֹ.
לְךָ וּלְךָ. לְךָ כִּי לְךָ.
לְךָ אַף לְךָ. לְךָ יְיָ הַמַּמְלָכָה.
כִּי לוֹ נָאֶה. כִּי לוֹ יָאֶה:

(*The Seder text continues on page 86.*)

The Kid of the Haggadah

There in the market place, bleating among the billy goats and nannies,
Wagging his thin little tail—as thin as my finger—
Stood the Kid—downcast, outcast, the leavings of a poor man's house,
Put up for sale without a bell, without even a ribbon, for just a couple of cents.

Not a single soul in the market paid him any attention,
For no one knew—not even the goldsmith, the sheep-shearer—
That this lonesome little Kid would enter the Haggadah
And his tale of woe become a mighty song.

But Daddy's face lit up,
He walked over to pat the Kid's forehead—and bought him.
And so began one of those songs
That people will sing for all history.

The Kid licked Daddy's hand,
Nuzzled him with his wet little nose;
And this, my brother, will make the first verse of the song:
"One only Kid, one only Kid, that my father bought for two zuzim."

It was a spring day, and the breezes danced;
Young girls winked and giggled, flashed their eyes;
While Daddy and the Kid walked into the Haggadah
To stand there together—small nose in large hand, large hand on small nose.

Four is the number of the matriarchs.

To find in the Haggadah—
So full already of miracles and marvels—
A peaceful place on the last page,
Where they can hug each other and cling to the edge of the story.

And this very Haggadah whispers,
"Join us . . . you're welcome here . . . you belong,
Among my pages full of smoke and blood,
Among the great and ancient tales I tell."

So I know the sea was not split in vain,
Deserts not crossed in vain—
If at the end of the story stand Daddy and the Kid
Looking forward and knowing their turn will come.

Nathan Alterman, translated by Arthur I. Waskow and Judy Spelman

* * *

חַד גַּדְיָא

An Only Kid

חַד גַּדְיָא, חַד גַּדְיָא, 𝄞 29
דִּזְבַן אַבָּא בִּתְרֵי זוּזֵי;
חַד גַּדְיָא, חַד גַּדְיָא,

וְאָתָא שׁוּנְרָא וְאָכַל לְגַדְיָא,
דִּזְבַן אַבָּא בִּתְרֵי זוּזֵי;
חַד גַּדְיָא, חַד גַּדְיָא.

וְאָתָא כַלְבָּא וְנָשַׁךְ לְשׁוּנְרָא,
דְּאָכַל לְגַדְיָא, דִּזְבַן אַבָּא בִּתְרֵי זוּזֵי;
חַד גַּדְיָא, חַד גַּדְיָא.

וְאָתָא חוּטְרָא וְהִכָּה לְכַלְבָּא,
דְּנָשַׁךְ לְשׁוּנְרָא, דְּאָכַל לְגַדְיָא,
דִּזְבַן אַבָּא בִּתְרֵי זוּזֵי;
חַד גַּדְיָא, חַד גַּדְיָא.

וְאָתָא נוּרָא וְשָׂרַף לְחוּטְרָא,
דְּהִכָּה לְכַלְבָּא, דְּנָשַׁךְ לְשׁוּנְרָא,
דְּאָכַל לְגַדְיָא, דִּזְבַן אַבָּא בִּתְרֵי זוּזֵי;
חַד גַּדְיָא, חַד גַּדְיָא.

וְאָתָא מַיָּא וְכָבָה לְנוּרָא,
דְּשָׂרַף לְחוּטְרָא, דְּהִכָּה לְכַלְבָּא,

דְּנָשַׁךְ לְשׁוּנְרָא, דְּאָכַל לְגַדְיָא,
דִּזְבַן אַבָּא בִּתְרֵי זוּזֵי;
חַד גַּדְיָא, חַד גַּדְיָא.

וְאָתָא תוֹרָא וְשָׁתָא לְמַיָּא,
דְּכָבָה לְנוּרָא, דְּשָׂרַף לְחוּטְרָא,
דְּהִכָּה לְכַלְבָּא, דְּנָשַׁךְ לְשׁוּנְרָא,
דְּאָכַל לְגַדְיָא, דִּזְבַן אַבָּא בִּתְרֵי זוּזֵי;
חַד גַּדְיָא, חַד גַּדְיָא.

וְאָתָא הַשּׁוֹחֵט וְשָׁחַט לְתוֹרָא,
דְּשָׁתָה לְמַיָּא, דְּכָבָה לְנוּרָא,
דְּשָׂרַף לְחוּטְרָא, דְּהִכָּה לְכַלְבָּא,
דְּנָשַׁךְ לְשׁוּנְרָא, דְּאָכַל לְגַדְיָא,
דִּזְבַן אַבָּא בִּתְרֵי זוּזֵי;
חַד גַּדְיָא, חַד גַּדְיָא.

וְאָתָא מַלְאַךְ הַמָּוֶת, וְשָׁחַט לַשּׁוֹחֵט,
דְּשָׁחַט לְתוֹרָא, דְּשָׁתָה לְמַיָּא,
דְּכָבָה לְנוּרָא, דְּשָׂרַף לְחוּטְרָא,
דְּהִכָּה לְכַלְבָּא, דְּנָשַׁךְ לְשׁוּנְרָא,
דְּאָכַל לְגַדְיָא, דִּזְבַן אַבָּא בִּתְרֵי זוּזֵי;
חַד גַּדְיָא, חַד גַּדְיָא.

וְאָתָא הַקָּדוֹשׁ בָּרוּךְ הוּא, וְשָׁחַט לְמַלְאַךְ הַמָּוֶת,
דְּשָׁחַט לַשּׁוֹחֵט, דְּשָׁחַט לְתוֹרָא,
דְּשָׁתָה לְמַיָּא, דְּכָבָה לְנוּרָא,
דְּשָׂרַף לְחוּטְרָא, דְּהִכָּה לְכַלְבָּא,
דְּנָשַׁךְ לְשׁוּנְרָא, דְּאָכַל לְגַדְיָא,
דִּזְבַן אַבָּא בִּתְרֵי זוּזֵי;
חַד גַּדְיָא, חַד גַּדְיָא.

An only kid, an only kid.

Chorus: My father bought for two zuzim *had gadya.*

1 Then came the cat
And ate the kid
Chorus

2 Then came the dog
And bit the cat
That ate the kid
Chorus

3 Then came the stick
And beat the dog
That bit the cat
That ate the kid
Chorus

4 Then came the fire
And burned the stick
That beat the dog
That bit the cat
That ate the kid
Chorus

5 Then came the water
And quenched the fire
That burned the stick
That beat the dog
That bit the cat
That ate the kid
Chorus

6 Then came the ox
And drank the water
That quenched the fire
That burned the stick
That beat the dog
That bit the cat
That ate the kid
Chorus

7 Then came the butcher
And killed the ox
That drank the water
That quenched the fire
That burned the stick
That beat the dog
That bit the cat
That ate the kid
Chorus

8 Then came the angel of death
And slew the butcher
That killed the ox
That drank the water
That quenched the fire
That burned the stick
That beat the dog
That bit the cat
That ate the kid
Chorus

9 Then came the Holy One, blessed be He,
And destroyed the angel of death
That slew the butcher
That killed the ox
That drank the water
That quenched the fire
That burned the stick
That beat the dog
That bit the cat
That ate the kid
Chorus

An only kid.

יהוה

וַיְהִי בַּחֲצִי הַלַּיְלָה

And It Came to Pass at Midnight

אָז רוֹב נִסִּים הִפְלֵאתָ בַּלַּיְלָה, בְּרֹאשׁ אַשְׁמוּרוֹת זֶה הַלַּיְלָה, גֵּר צֶדֶק נִצַּחְתּוֹ
כְּנֶחֱלַק לוֹ לַיְלָה, וַיְהִי בַּחֲצִי הַלַּיְלָה:

קָרֵב יוֹם אֲשֶׁר הוּא לֹא יוֹם וְלֹא לַיְלָה, רָם הוֹדַע כִּי לְךָ הַיּוֹם אַף לְךָ הַלַּיְלָה, 𝄞 30
שׁוֹמְרִים הַפְקֵד לְעִירְךָ כָּל הַיּוֹם וְכָל הַלַּיְלָה, תָּאִיר כְּאוֹר יוֹם חֶשְׁכַּת לַיְלָה,
וַיְהִי בַּחֲצִי הַלַּיְלָה:

(All read the indented lines in unison.)

Unto God let praise be brought
For the wonders He has wrought
    At the solemn hour of midnight.
All the earth was sunk in night
When God said, "Let there be light!"
    Thus the day was formed from midnight.
To the Patriarch, God revealed
A true faith, so long concealed
    By the darkness of the midnight.
But this truth was long obscured
By the slavery endured
    In the black Egyptian midnight.
Then the people God had freed
Pledged themselves His law to heed,
    And this came to pass at midnight.
O You, Guardian of the Right,
Lead us onward to the light
    From the darkness of the midnight.
When no longer shall the foe
From oppressed wring cries of woe
    In the darkness of the midnight.
A day will come, a day draws nigh
That is neither day nor night.
Make known the truth, God, from on high—
    To You belong both day and night.
    A DAY WILL COME, A DAY DRAWS NIGH
    THAT IS NEITHER DAY NOR NIGHT.
    MAKE KNOWN THE TRUTH, GOD, FROM ON HIGH—
    TO YOU BELONG BOTH DAY AND NIGHT.

Translation from Hebrew of Jannai, by Henry Berkowitz

(The Seder text continues on page 91.)

שַׂחֲקִי

Credo

𝄞 31 Laugh at all my dreams, my dearest,
Laugh and I repeat anew
That I still believe in man
As I still believe in you;
That I still believe in man
As I still believe in you.

By the passion of our spirit
Shall our ancient bonds be shed.
Let the soul be given freedom,
Let the body have its bread!
Let the soul be given freedom,
Let the body have its bread!

For my soul is not yet sold
To the golden calf of scorn;
For I still believe in man,
And the spirit in him born.
For I still believe in man,
And the spirit in him born.

Life and love and strength and action
In our heart and blood shall beat,
And our hopes shall be both heaven
And the earth beneath our feet.
And our hopes shall be both heaven
And the earth beneath our feet.

שַׂחֲקִי, שַׂחֲקִי עַל הַחֲלוֹמוֹת,
זוּ אֲנִי הַחוֹלֵם שָׂח,
שַׂחֲקִי כִּי בָאָדָם אַאֲמִין,
כִּי עוֹדֶנִּי מַאֲמִין בָּךְ.

כִּי עוֹד נַפְשִׁי דְּרוֹר שׁוֹאֶפֶת –
לֹא מְכַרְתִּיהָ לְעֵגֶל פָּז,
כִּי עוֹד אַאֲמִין גַּם בָּאָדָם,
גַּם בְּרוּחוֹ, רוּחַ עָז.

אַאֲמִינָה גַם בֶּעָתִיד,
אַף אִם יִרְחַק זֶה הַיּוֹם,
אַךְ בֹּא יָבוֹא – יִשְּׂאוּ שָׁלוֹם
אָז וּבְרָכָה לְאֹם מִלְאֹם.

Translation from Hebrew of Saul Chernichovsky, by Maurice Samuel

* * *

נִרְצָה

NIRTZAH, CONCLUSION

כּוֹס הַרְצָאָה

Kos Hartza-ah, the Fourth Cup—the Cup of Acceptance

Leader

As our Seder draws to an end, we take up our cups of wine. The Redemption is not yet complete. The fourth cup recalls us to our covenant with the Eternal One, to the tasks that still await us as a people called to the

לשנה
הבא
בירושל

service of God, to a great purpose for which the people of Israel lives: The preservation and affirmation of hope.

שֶׁנֶּאֱמַר וְלָקַחְתִּי אֶתְכֶם לִי לְעָם:

Group

Exodus 6:7 As it is written: "And *I will take you* to be my people."

בָּרוּךְ אַתָּה יְיָ אֱלֹהֵינוּ מֶלֶךְ הָעוֹלָם בּוֹרֵא פְּרִי הַגָּפֶן:

Baruḥ Atah Adonai Eloheinu Meleḥ ha-olam borei p'ri ha-gafen.

We praise Thee, our God, Sovereign of all Existence, Who has created the fruit of the vine.

(*All drink the fourth cup of wine.*)

Leader

𝄞 32 THE SEDER SERVICE NOW CONCLUDES:
ITS RITES OBSERVED IN FULL,
ITS PURPOSES REVEALED.

Group

THIS PRIVILEGE WE SHARE WILL EVER BE RENEWED.
UNTIL GOD'S PLAN IS KNOWN IN FULL,
GOD'S HIGHEST BLESSING SEALED:

חֲסַל סִדּוּר פֶּסַח כְּהִלְכָתוֹ,
כְּכָל מִשְׁפָּטוֹ וְחֻקָּתוֹ.
כַּאֲשֶׁר זָכִינוּ לְסַדֵּר אוֹתוֹ,
כֵּן נִזְכֶּה לַעֲשׂוֹתוֹ.
זָךְ שׁוֹכֵן מְעוֹנָה,
קוֹמֵם קְהַל עֲדַת מִי מָנָה.
בְּקָרוֹב נַהֵל נִטְעֵי כַנָּה,
פְּדוּיִם לְצִיּוֹן בְּרִנָּה.

Leader

PEACE!

Group

PEACE FOR US! FOR EVERYONE!

Leader

FOR ALL PEOPLE, THIS, OUR HOPE:

Group

NEXT YEAR IN JERUSALEM!
NEXT YEAR, MAY ALL BE FREE!

(*Next year in Jerusalem is ever the hope of our people. Still we affirm that all people will rejoice together in the Zion of love and peace.*)

𝄞 33 L'SHANAH HABA-AH BIRUSHALA-YIM!

לְשָׁנָה הַבָּאָה בִּירוּשָׁלָיִם:

Next year in Jerusalem!

אַדִּיר הוּא

God of Might

אַדִּיר הוּא. אַדִּיר הוּא. יִבְנֶה בֵיתוֹ 𝄞 34
בְּקָרוֹב. בִּמְהֵרָה. בִּמְהֵרָה. בְּיָמֵינוּ
בְּקָרוֹב. אֵל בְּנֵה. אֵל בְּנֵה. בְּנֵה
בֵיתְךָ בְּקָרוֹב:

God of Might, God of Right,
We would bow before Thee,
Sing Thy praise in these days,
Celebrate Thy glory,
As we hear, year by year,
Freedom's wondrous story.

בָּחוּר הוּא. גָּדוֹל הוּא. דָּגוּל הוּא.
יִבְנֶה בֵיתוֹ בְּקָרוֹב. בִּמְהֵרָה. בִּמְהֵרָה.
בְּיָמֵינוּ בְּקָרוֹב. אֵל בְּנֵה. אֵל בְּנֵה.
בְּנֵה בֵיתְךָ בְּקָרוֹב:

Now as erst, when Thou first
Mad'st the proclamation,
Warning loud ev'ry proud,
Ev'ry tyrant nation,
We Thy fame still proclaim,
Bend in adoration.

נָאוֹר הוּא. סַגִּיב הוּא. עִזּוּז הוּא.
יִבְנֶה בֵיתוֹ בְּקָרוֹב. בִּמְהֵרָה. בִּמְהֵרָה.
בְּיָמֵינוּ בְּקָרוֹב. אֵל בְּנֵה. אֵל בְּנֵה.
בְּנֵה בֵיתְךָ בְּקָרוֹב:

Be with all who in thrall
To their task are driven;
In Thy power speed the hour
When their chains are riven;
Earth around will resound
Joyful hymns to heaven.

פּוֹדֶה הוּא. צַדִּיק הוּא. קָדוֹשׁ הוּא.
יִבְנֶה בֵיתוֹ בְּקָרוֹב. בִּמְהֵרָה. בִּמְהֵרָה.
בְּיָמֵינוּ בְּקָרוֹב. אֵל בְּנֵה. אֵל בְּנֵה.
בְּנֵה בֵיתְךָ בְּקָרוֹב:

(*An alternative English text will be found on page 122.*)

SONGS

1 KADEISH UR'ḤATZ / ORDER OF THE SEDER

Malcolm H. Stern *Babylonian Melody*

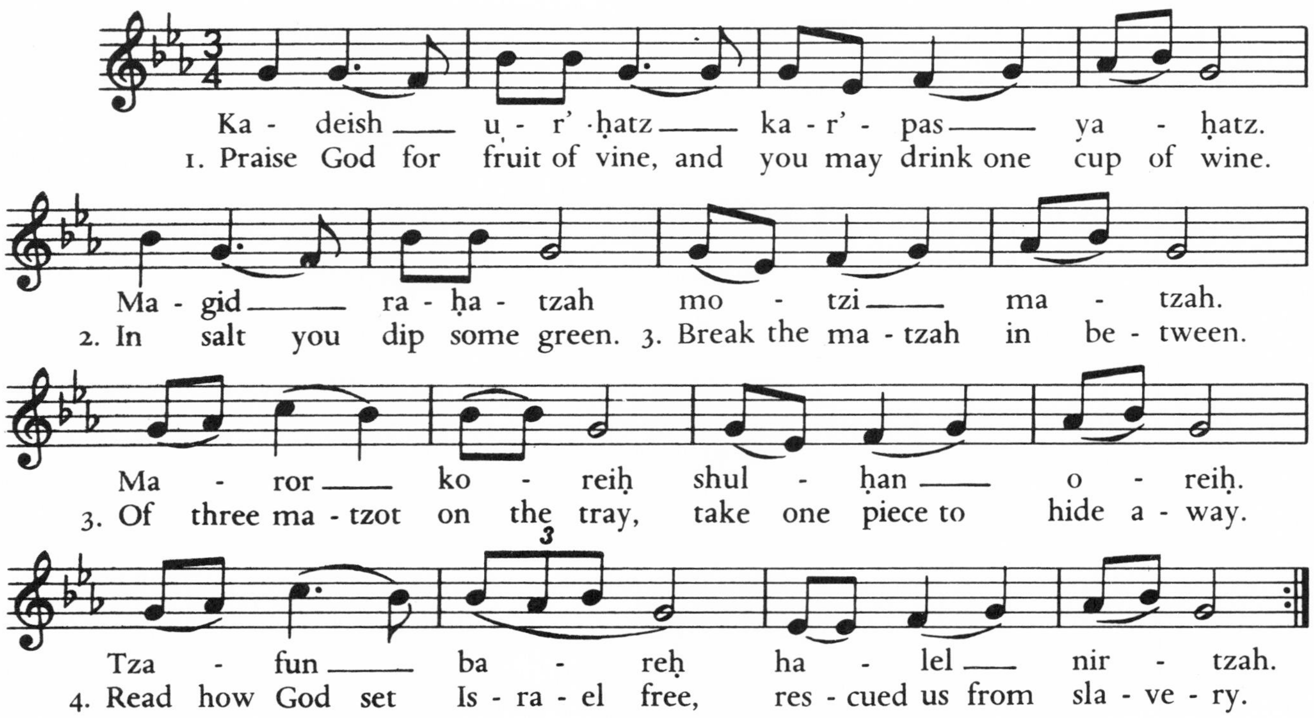
Ka - deish u - r' -ḥatz ka - r' - pas ya - ḥatz.
1. Praise God for fruit of vine, and you may drink one cup of wine.
Ma - gid ra - ḥa - tzah mo - tzi ma - tzah.
2. In salt you dip some green. 3. Break the ma - tzah in be - tween.
Ma - ror ko - reiḥ shul - ḥan o - reiḥ.
3. Of three ma - tzot on the tray, take one piece to hide a - way.
Tza - fun ba - reḥ ha - lel nir - tzah.
4. Read how God set Is - ra - el free, res - cued us from sla - ve - ry.

5. Matzah you bless and eat.
6. With bitter herbs, ḥaroset sweet.
7. At last the meal takes place.
8. But before you say the grace,
   find the afikoman.
9. Bring the supper to its end.
10. Then recite the psalms of praise,
    final thanks to God we raise.

BLESSING OVER THE LIGHTS

A. W. Binder

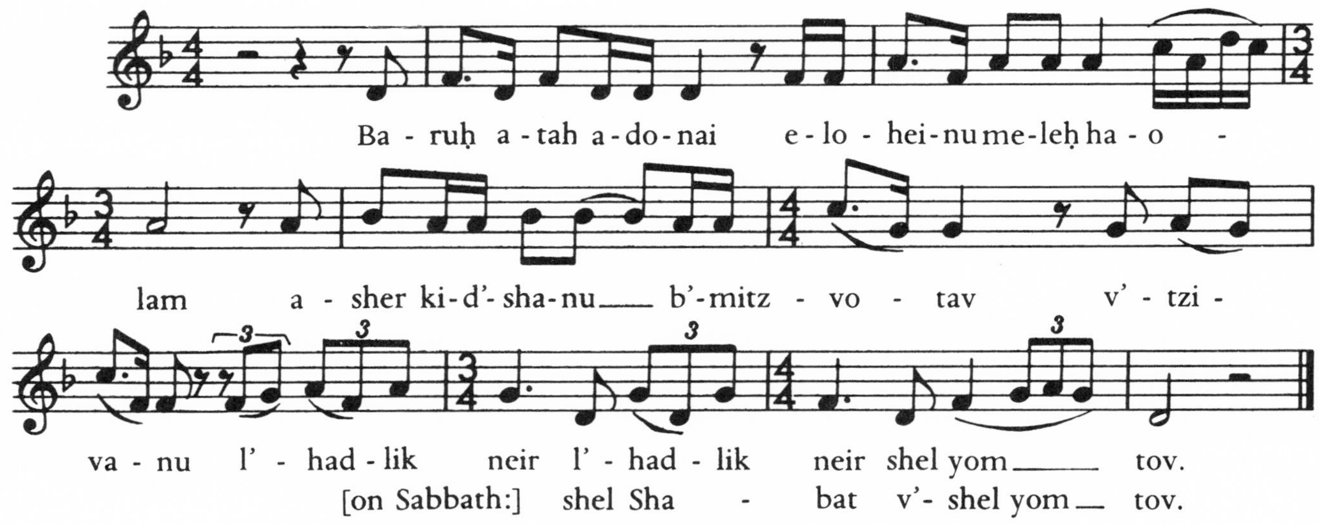
Ba - ruḥ a - tah a - do - nai e - lo - hei - nu me - leḥ ha - o -
lam a - sher ki - d'- sha - nu b'-mitz - vo - tav v' - tzi -
va - nu l' - had - lik neir l' - had - lik neir shel yom tov.
[on Sabbath:] shel Sha - bat v'- shel yom tov.

BLESSING OVER THE LIGHTS

3

Max Janowski

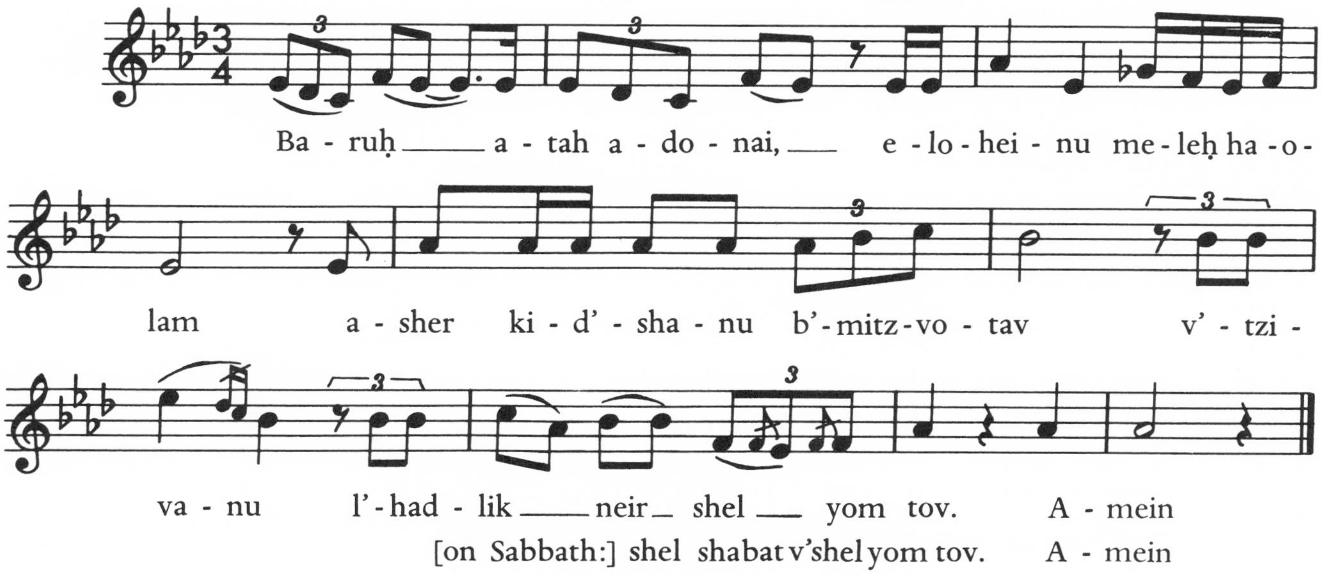
Ba - ruḥ a - tah a - do - nai, e - lo - hei - nu me - leḥ ha - o -
lam a - sher ki - d' - sha - nu b'- mitz - vo - tav v' - tzi -
va - nu l' - had - lik neir shel yom tov. A - mein
[on Sabbath:] shel shabat v'shel yom tov. A - mein

4

VAY'ḤULU

Genesis 2:1–4

From "What Is Torah?"—Judith K. Eisenstein

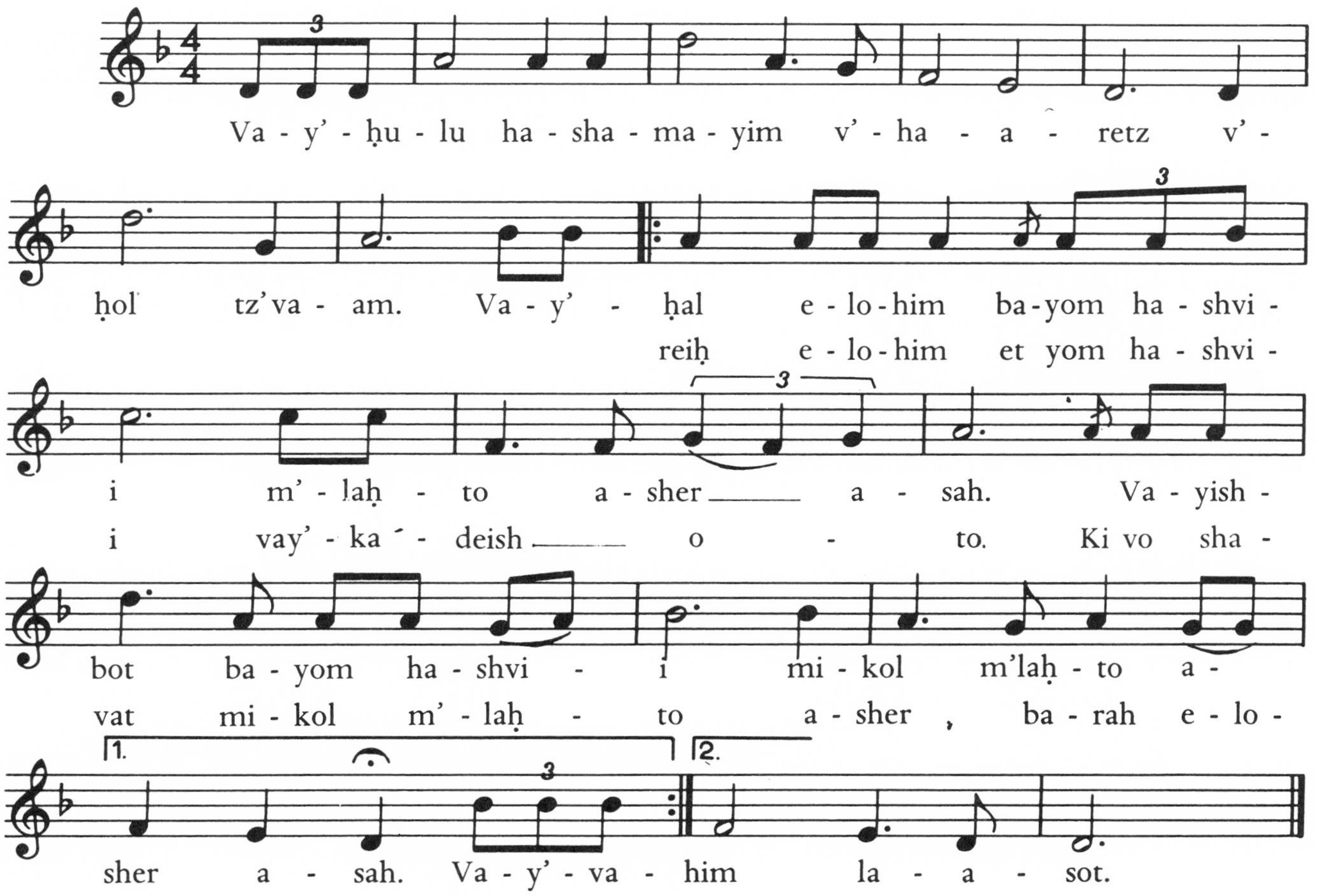
Va - y' - ḥu - lu ha - sha - ma - yim v' - ha - a - retz v' -
ḥol tz'va - am. Va - y' - ḥal e - lo - him ba - yom ha - shvi -
reiḥ e - lo - him et yom ha - shvi -
i m' - laḥ - to a - sher a - sah. Va - yish -
i vay' - ka - deish o - to. Ki vo sha -
bot ba - yom ha - shvi - i mi - kol m'laḥ - to a -
vat mi - kol m' - laḥ - to a - sher , ba - rah e - lo -
1.
2.
sher a - sah. Va - y' - va - him la - a - sot.

Sav - ri ma-ra-nan v' - ra-bo - tai. Ba - ruḥ a - tah a-do-nai e-lo-
hei - nu me-leḥ ha-o-lam bo - rei ___ p' - ri ha-ga - fen. A - mein Ba -
ruḥ a - tah a-do-nai e-lo - hei - nu me - leḥ ha - o - lam a -
sher ba-ḥar ba-nu mi - kol am ___ v'-ro - m'-ma-nu mi - kol la-shon _ v'-kid'-
sha-nu b'-mitz-vo-tav. ___ Va-ti - tein la-nu a - do - nai e - lo-hei-nu b'a - ha -
vah ___ (sha-ba-tot lim-nu-ḥa u-) mo-a - dim l'-sim-ḥa __ ḥa-gim u-z'ma-nim l'-sa-
son. __ Et (yom ha - sha-bat ha-zeh v'et) yom ḥag ha - ma-tzot ha-zeh ___ z'-
man ḥei-ru - tei-nu (b'a-ha-vah) mi-krah ko-desh zei-ḥer li-tzi - at mitz-rai-yim. Ki
va - nu va - ḥar-tah v'- o - ta - nu ki -dash-ta mi - kol ha - a - mim (v'-sha-
bat) u-mo-a - dei kod - sh' - ḥa (b' - a-ha-vah uv'-ra-tzon) b'-sim - ḥa uv'-sa-son
hin - ḥal - ta - nu. Ba - ruḥ a - tah a - do - nai m'-ka -
deish yis-ra - eil v' - ha-z'ma - nim. Ba - ruḥ a - tah a-do-nai e - lo -
(ha-sha-bat v'yis-ra - eil v'ha-z'ma-nim).

hei - nu me- leḥ ha - o - lam sheh - heh - ḥeh - ya nu v' -
kiy' - ma - nu v' - ḥi - gi - a - nu la - z'man ha - zeh.

6 SONG OF SONGS

Song of Songs 2:10–12 *Traditional nigun*

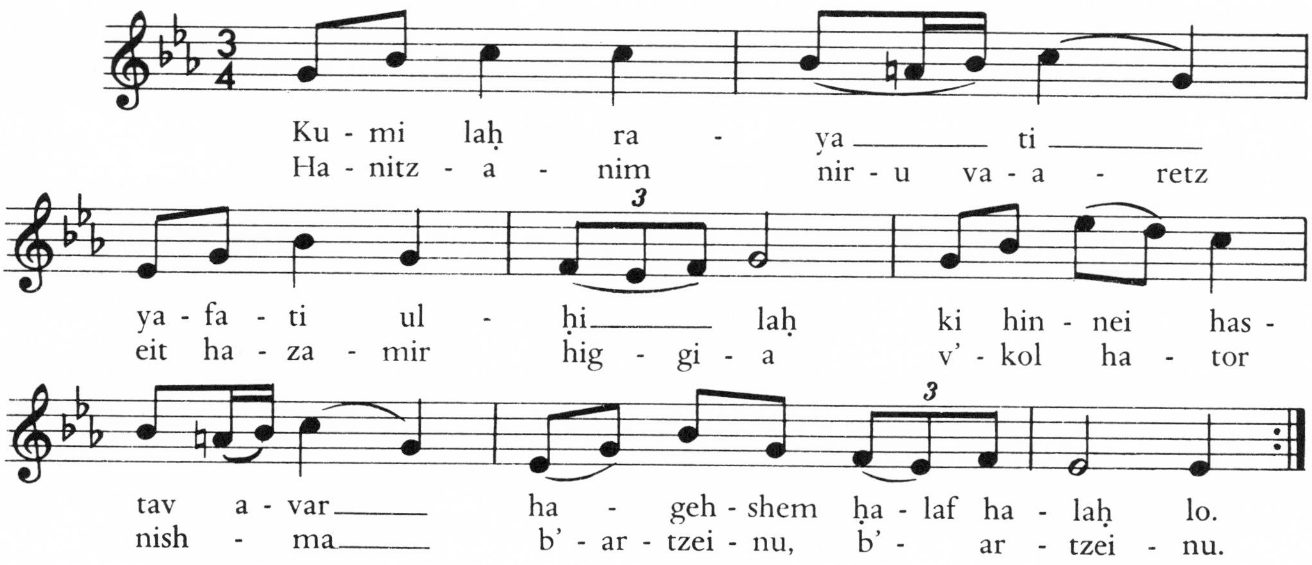
Ku - mi laḥ ra - ya ti
Ha - nitz - a - nim nir - u va - a - retz
ya - fa - ti ul - ḥi laḥ ki hin - nei has -
eit ha - za - mir hig - gi - a v' - kol ha - tor
tav a - var ha - geh - shem ḥa - laf ha - laḥ lo.
nish - ma b' - ar - tzei - nu, b' - ar - tzei - nu.

7

HA LAḤMA

Traditional "Shir Hamaalot" tune

Ha __ laḥ - ma an - yah di - a - ḥa - lu a - ha - va - ta - nah b' - ar -
ah d' - mitz - ra - yim. Kol __ diḥ - fin yei - tei
v' - yei - ḥul, kol ditz - riḥ yei - tei v' - yif - saḥ. Ha -
sha - tah ha - ḥa l' - sha - nah ha - ba - ah b' - ar - ah d' -
yis - ra - eil, ha - sha - tah av - dei l' - sha - nah ha - ba - ah l' -
sha - nah ha - ba - ah b' - nei ḥo - rin.

Israeli

3. She-b'-ḥol ha-lei-lot ein a-nu mat-bi-lin a-fi-lu pa-am e-ḥat.
   Ha-lai-lah ha-zeh, ha-lai-lah ha-zeh sh'-tei f'a-a-mim.
4. She-b'-ḥol ha-lei-lot a-nu oḥ-lin bein yosh-vin u-vein m'-su-bin.
   Ha-lai-lah ha-zeh, ha-lai-lah ha-zeh ku-la-nu m'-su-bin.

9 MA NISHTANA

10 AVADIM HAYINU

S. Postolsky

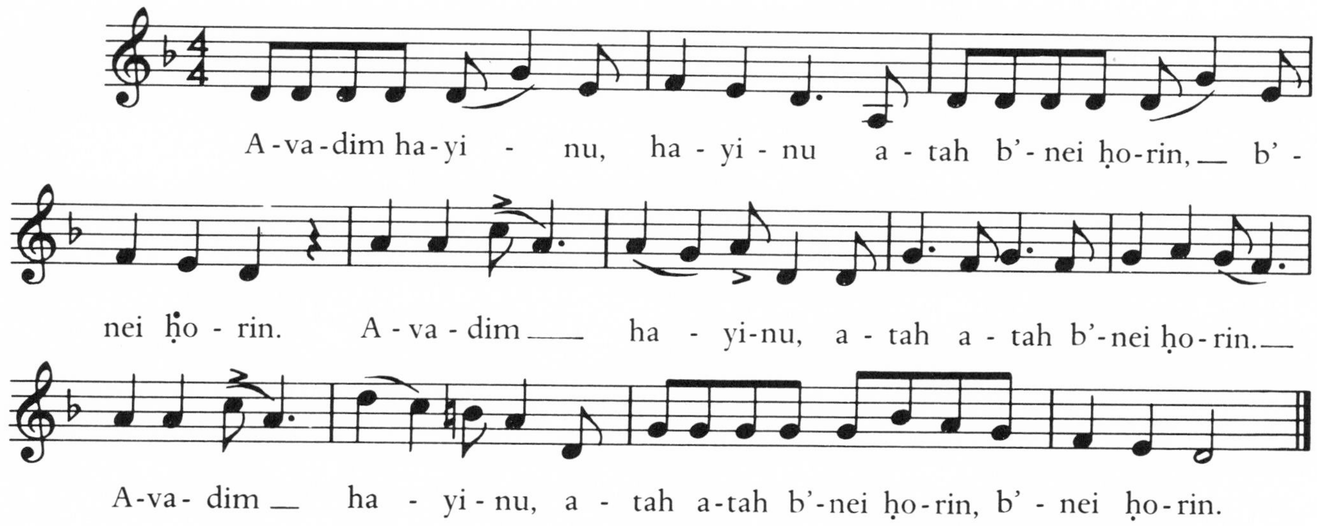
A-va-dim ha-yi - nu, ha - yi - nu a - tah b'-nei ḥo-rin, b'-
nei ḥo - rin. A - va - dim ha - yi-nu, a - tah a - tah b'-nei ḥo-rin.
A-va- dim ha - yi - nu, a - tah a-tah b'-nei ḥo-rin, b' - nei ḥo-rin.

11 V'HI SHEAMDAH

V' - hi she-am - dah la - a - vo - tei - nu v' - la -
nu. V' - hi she-am - dah la-a - vo - tei - nu v' - la -
nu. She - lo e - ḥad bil - vad a - mad a - lei - nu l' -
ḥa - lo - tei - nu. She - lo e - ḥad bil - vad a - mad a - lei - nu l' -
ha - lo - tei - nu. V'ha-ka-dosh ba-ruḥ hu ma - tzi - lei - nu
ma - tzi - lei - nu mi - ya - dam. V' - hi she - am -
dah la - a - vo - tei - nu v' - la - nu.

12

V'HI SHEAMDAH

Ḥasidic

V' - hi she - am - dah, v'hi she - am - dah la - a - vo - tei - nu v' - la - nu. V' -
hi she - am - dah, v'hi she - am - dah la - a - vo - tei - nu v' - la - nu. She -
lo e - ḥad bi - l' - vad a - mad a - lei - nu l' - ḥa - lo - tei - nu. She - e -
la she - b' - ḥol___ dor va - dor om - dim a - lei - nu l' - ḥa - lo - tei - nu.
V'ha - ka - dosh ba - ruḥ hu ma - tzi - lei - nu mi - ya - dam.

13

DAYEINU

I - lu ho - tzi ho - tzi - a - nu, ho - tzi - a - nu mi - mitz - ra - yim,
ho - tzi - a - nu mi - mitz - ra - yim da - yei - nu.
(Chorus) Da - da - yei - nu,___ da - da - yei - nu,___ da - da - yei - nu, da -
1., 2.
yei - nu da - yei - nu da - yei - nu.
3.
yei - nu da - yei - nu.

2. I-lu na-tan, na-tan la-nu, na-tan la-nu et ha-sha-bat, na-tan la-nu et ha-sha-bat, dayeinu. (Chorus).
3. I-lu na-tan, na-tan la-nu, na-tan la-nu et ha-to-rah, na-tan la-nu et ha-to-rah, dayeinu. (Chorus.)

English words: Mrs. Leo H. Honor

Yemenite

1. Pe - saḥ, Pe - saḥ time is here. Pe - saḥ,
E - ḥad mi yo - dei - ah? E - ḥad a -
Pe - saḥ time is here. With its ma - tzot and its wine
ni yo - dei - ah. E - ḥad e - lo - hei - nu, e -
we will feast and we will dine. La la la la la la la la La
lo - hei - nu, e - lo - hei - nu, e - lo - hei - nu, e - lo - hei - nu, e -
la la la la la la la la Pe - saḥ,
lo - hei - nu she - ba - sha - ma - yim
Pe - saḥ time is here. Pe - saḥ, Pe - saḥ time is here.
u - va - a - retz, she - ba - sha - ma - yim u - va - a - retz.

2. Pesaḥ, Pesaḥ time is here.
Pesaḥ, Pesaḥ time is here.
Four questions I will ask,
And hear the story of our past
Pesaḥ, Pesaḥ time is here.

3. Pesaḥ, Pesaḥ time is here.
Pesaḥ, Pesaḥ time is here.
The bitter herbs I will taste
And eat ḥaroset in great haste.
Pesaḥ, Pesaḥ time is here.

4. Pesaḥ, Pesaḥ time is here.
Pesaḥ, Pesaḥ time is here.
The afikoman I will steal,
And then how happy I will feel.
Pesaḥ, Pesaḥ time is here.

5. Pesah, Pesaḥ time is here.
Pesaḥ, Pesaḥ time is here.
Many songs we shall sing;
With Ḥad Gadya our voices ring.
Pesaḥ, Pesaḥ time is here.

15 V'NOMAR L'FANAV

Ḥasidic

V' - no - mar l' - fa - nav shi - ra___ ḥa - da - sha. V' - no - mar l' - fa - nav
1. 2.
shir - ra ḥa - da - sha. V' shi - ra - ḥa - da - sha, ha - l'- lu - yah.___
1. 2.
Ha - l' -lu - yah. Ha - l' -lu - yah. Ha - l'- lu - yah. Ha - l'- lu - yah.

16 HAL'LUYAH

Psalm 113

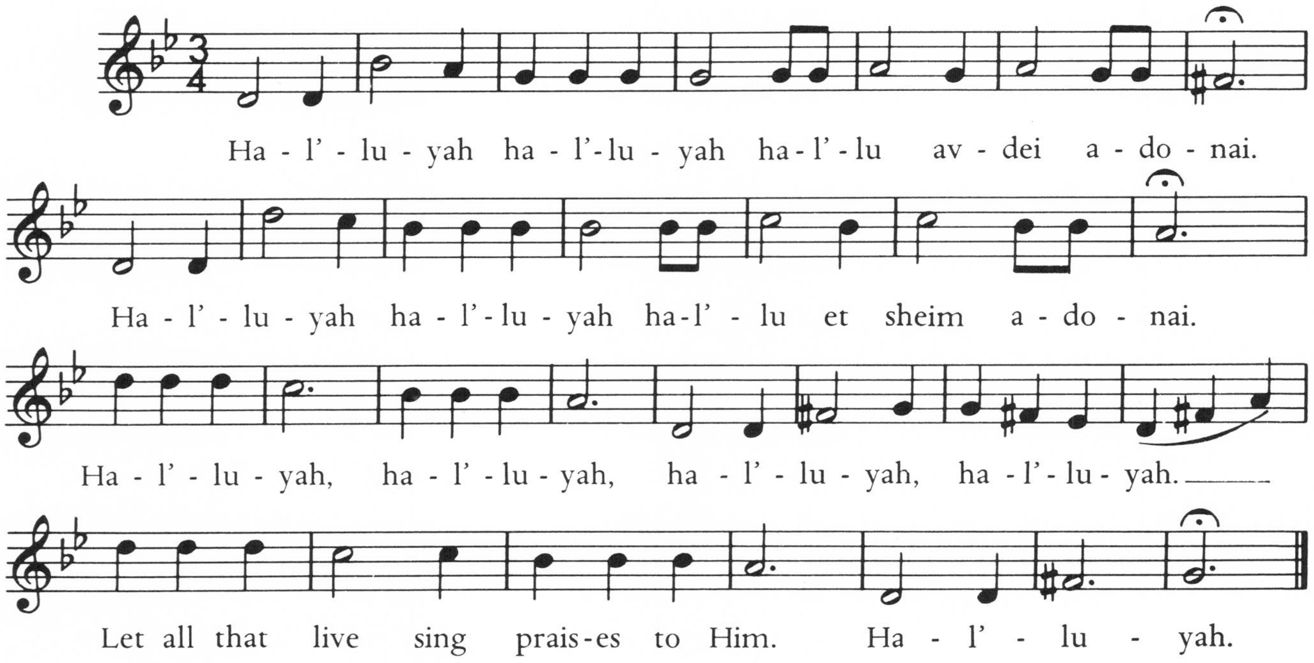
Ha - l' - lu - yah ha - l'- lu - yah ha - l' - lu av - dei a - do - nai.
Ha - l' - lu - yah ha - l' - lu - yah ha - l' - lu et sheim a - do - nai.
Ha - l' - lu - yah, ha - l' - lu - yah, ha - l' - lu - yah, ha - l'- lu - yah.___
Let all that live sing prais - es to Him. Ha - l' - lu - yah.

17

HALLEL

Psalm 113

Ha - l' - lu av - dei a - do - nai. Ha - l' - lu et
Mi - miz - raḥ she - mesh ad m' - vo - o m' - ḥu - lal et
sheim a - do - nai y' - hi sheim a - do - nai m' - vo - raḥ
sheim a - do - nai. Ram al kol go - yim a - do - nai
1.
me - a - tah v' - ad o - lam. Ha - l' - lu -
al ha - sha - ma - yim k' - vo - do.
2.
yah. Ha - l' - lu - yah.

18

B'TZEIT YISRAEIL

Psalm 114

Israeli

B' - tzeit yis-ra - eil___ mi - mitz-ra - yim beit ya-a - kov___

mei - am lo - eiz. B' - tzeit yis-ra - eil___ mi - mitz-ra - yim beit ya-a - kov___

mei - am lo - eiz. Ha y'-tah Ha y'-tah___ y'-hu - dah l'-kod - sho___

yis - ra - eil___ mam - sh' - lo - tav. Ha - yam ha-yam ra -

ah___ va-ya - nos___ ha - yar-dein yi - sov___ l' - a - hor.

19

HALLEL (A ROUND)

Psalm 114

Psalm 126

Shir ___ ha - ma - a - lot b' - shuv _ a - do - nai ___
Shu - vah a - do - nai ___ et ___ sh'- vi - tei - nu
et shi - vat tzi - on ha - yi - nu k' - ḥol - mim. ___ Az ___ yi -
ka - a - fi - kim ___ ba - ne - gev. Ha -
ma - lei s' - ḥok ___ pi - nu ___ ul' - sho - nei - nu ri -
zor - im b' - di - mah ___ b' - ri - nah ___ yik - tzo -
nah. Az ___ yom - ru va - go - yim ___ hig - dil a - do -
ru. Ha - loḥ yei - leḥ u - va - ḥo ___ no - sei ___
nai ___ la - a - sot im ei - leh. Hig - dil a - do - nai ___
me - sheḥ ha - za - rah. Bo ___ ya - vo
la - a - sot i - ma - nu ha - yi - nu s' - mei - ḥim.
b'ri - nah ___ no - sei ___ a - lu - mo - tav.

Leader
Group, then Leader
Ra - bo - tai n'-va - reiḥ Y' - hi shem a - do - nai m'-vo-raḥ mei-a-
Leader
tah v'-ad o - lam. Bir - shut ma-ra - nan v'-ra - ba-nan v'-ra - bo-tai n'-va -
Group, then Leader
reiḥ e-lo- hei - nu she - a - ḥal - nu mi - she - lo. Ba -
ruḥ e-lo-hei - nu she - a - ḥal-nu mi - she-lo uv'-tu - vo ḥa - yi -
Group
nu. Ba - ruḥ hu u - va - ruḥ sh' - mo. Ba -
ruḥ a - tah a - do - nai e - lo - hei - nu me-leḥ ha- o - lam ha -
zan et ha - o - lam ku - lo b'- tu - vo b' - ḥein b'-ḥe-sed uv' -
ra-ha-mim hu no - tein le - hem l'-hol ba-sar
ki l'- o - lam has - do uv' - tu - vo ha-ga - dol ta -
mid lo ḥa - sar la - nu v' - al yeḥ-sar la - nu ma - zon l' - o -
lam va - ed. Ba - a - vur sh'-mo ha-ga - dol ki hu eil

zan um'-far-neis la - kol u-mei-tiv la-kol u-mei-
ḥin ma-zon l' - ḥol b'ri-yo-tav a - sher ba-rah. Ba-
ruḥ a-tah a-do-nai ha - zan et ha-kol.
Leader
Uv'-nei y'-ru-sha-la-yim ir ha - ko - desh bim-hei-ra b'-ya-
mei-nu Ba-ruḥ a-tah A-do - nai
Group
Bo-neh b'-ra-ḥa-mav y' - ru-sha-la-yim. A-mein.
Leader
B' - yom ḥag ha-ma-tzot ha - zeh zoḥ-
3
rei-nu a-do-nai e-lo-hei-nu bo l'-to-vah. A-mein U-fak-
Group
Leader
V'-
dei-nu vo liv' - ra - ḥah. A - mein.
ho-shi-ei - nu vo l' - ḥa-yim A - mein.
Group
1. Ha-ra-ḥa-man hu yim-loḥ a-lei-nu l'-o-lam va-ed.

2. Ha-ra-ḥa-man hu y'-far-n'sei-nu b'-ḥa-vod.

3. (On the Sabbath:) Ha-ra-ḥa-man hu yan-ḥi-lei-nu yom she-ku-lo sha-bat um'-nu-ḥah l'-ḥa-yei ha-o-la-mim.

4. Ha-ra-ḥa-man hu y'-za-kei-nu li-mot ha-ma-shi-ah ul'-ha-yei ha-o-lam ha-bah.

5. Ha-ra-ḥa-man hu yish-laḥ b'-ra-ḥah m'-ru-bah ba-ba-yit ha-zeh v'-al shul-ḥan zeh she-a-ḥal-nu a-lav.

6. Ha-ra-ḥa-man hu y'-va-reiḥ o-ta-nu v'-et kol a-sher la-nu k'mo she-nit-bar'-ḥu a-vo-tei-nu av-ra-ham yitz-ḥak v'- ya-a-kov ba-kol mi-kol kol.

M. Helfman

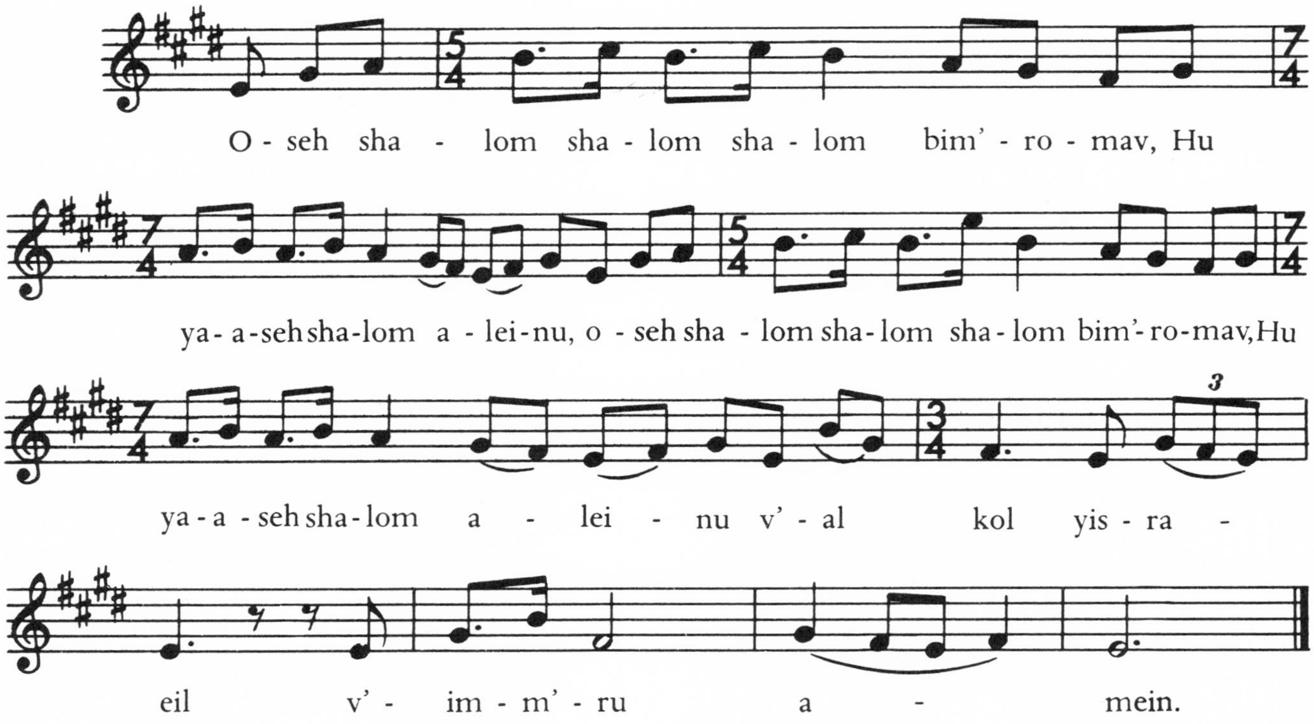

Psalm 29:11

Ray Cook

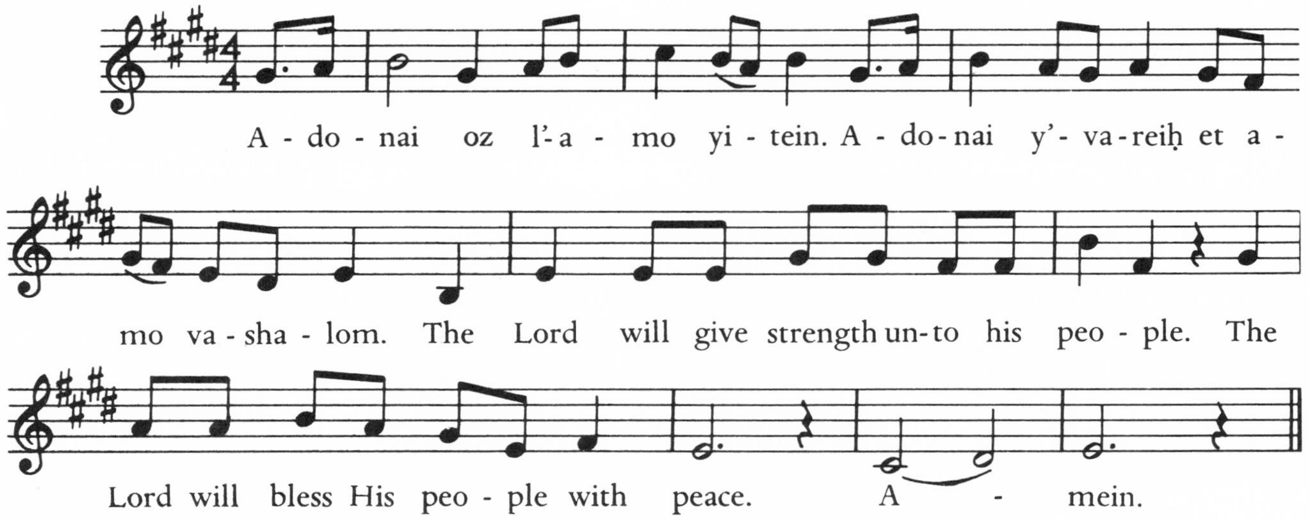

A - do - nai oz l'- a - mo yi - tein. A - do- nai y'- va-reiḥ et a -
mo va - sha - lom. The Lord will give strength un-to his peo - ple. The
Lord will bless His peo - ple with peace. A - mein.

EILIYAHU HANAVI

Ei - li - ya - hu ha - na - vi, ei - li - ya - hu ha - tish - bi,

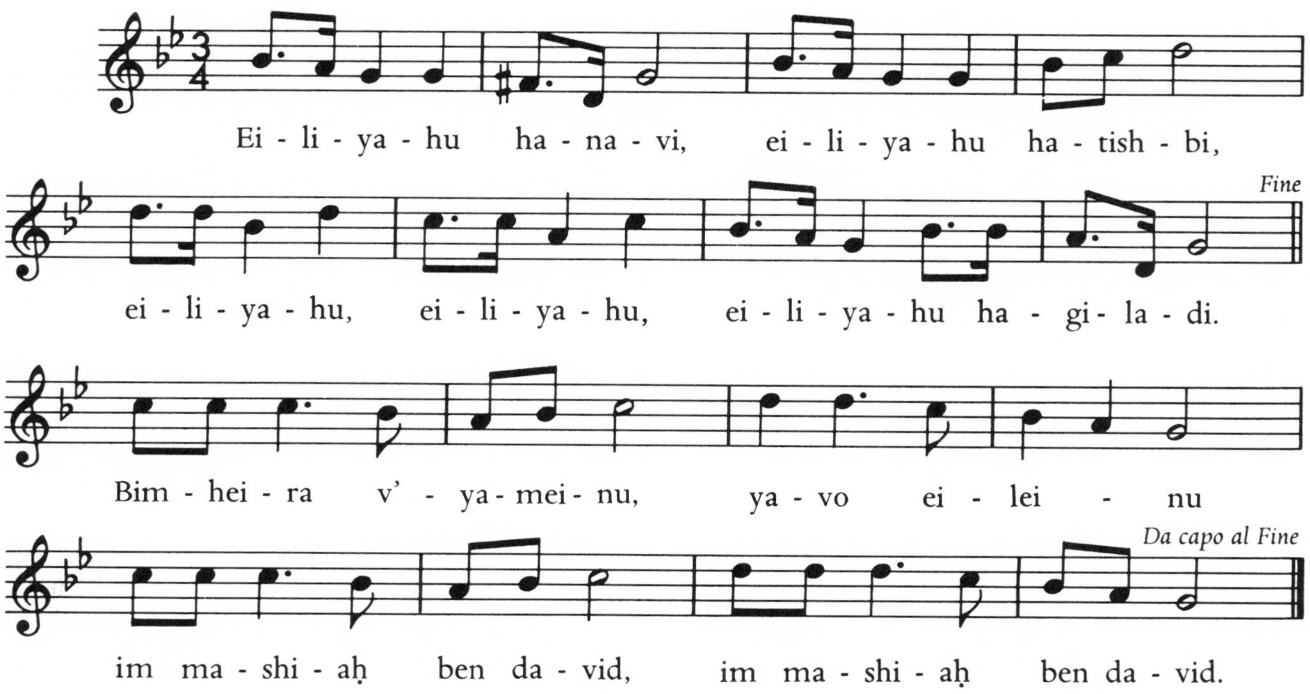

Fine

23

HAL'LU ET ADONAI KOL GOYIM

Ha - l' - lu et a - do - nai __ kol go - yim. Sha - b' - ḥu

hu kol ha - u - mim. Ki ga - var a - lei - nu ḥas -

do v' - e - met a - do - nai l' - o - lam. Ha - l' - lu - yah.

24 HODU LADONAI

Psalm 118:1–4

Loewenstamm

Refrain
Ho - du la - do - nai ki tov, ki l' - o - lam ḥas - do.
1. Yo - mar nah yis - ra - eil, ki l' - o - lam ḥas - do.
2. Yom - ru nah beit a - ha - ron, ki l' - o - lam ḥas - do.
3. Yom - ru nah yi - rei a - do - nai, ki l' - o - lam ḥas - do.

24A ANA ADONAI

Psalm 118:25

after Loewenstamm

25 PITḤU LI / Open Up, O Gates

Psalm 118:19, 17

Pit - ḥu li sha - a - rei tze - dek a - vo — vam o - de -
yah. Lo a - mut ki — eḥ - yeh — v'a - sa - peir ma - a - sei
yah. O - pen up, O gates — of right - eous - ness that we may
day which God has or - dained for us. For we were
en - ter and sing Thy praise. To Thee, O God, does Is - ra - el's
des - tined of old. We lift our voice, our souls — with -
song a - rise — won - drous in our eyes. This is the
in re - joice. His end - less praise be told.
1.
2.

26 AM YISRAEIL ḤAI

Folksong

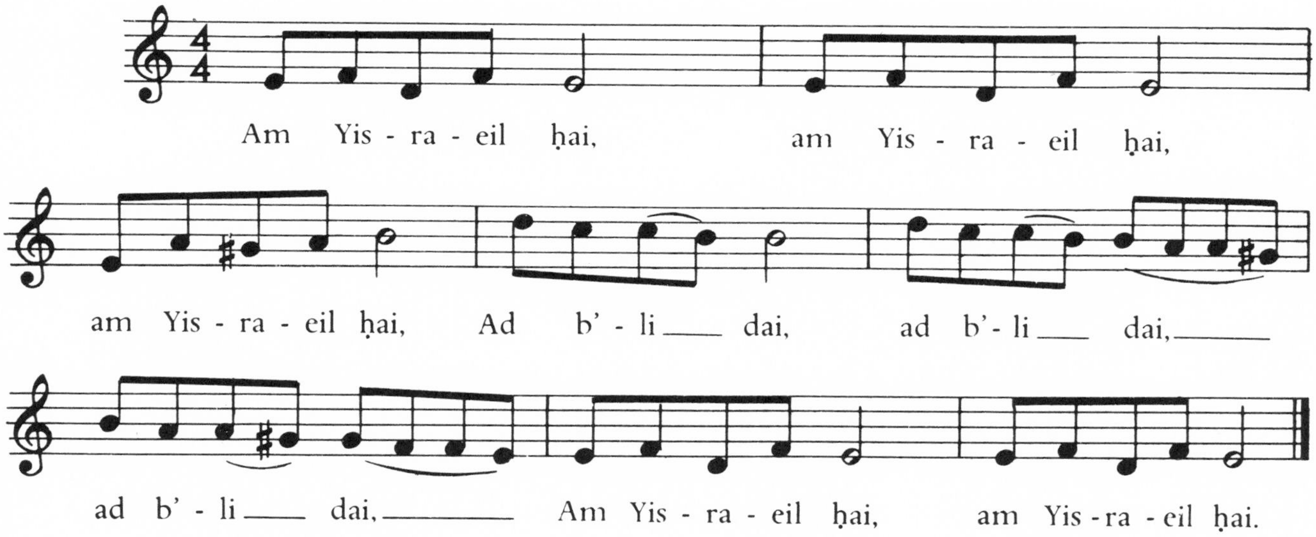

27 EḤAD MI YODEAH

1. E - ḥad mi yo - dei - ah? E - ḥad a - ni yo - dei - ah.
2. Sh' - na - yim mi yo - dei - ah? Sh'na - yim a - ni yo - dei - ah. Sh' -
(Omit . . . .) E -
nei lu - ḥot ha - br'it, sh' - nei lu - ḥot ha - br'it, e -
ḥad e - lo - hei - nu she - ba - sha - ma - yim u - va - a - retz.
ḥad e - lo - hei - nu she - ba - sha - ma - yim u - va - a - retz.

3. Sh'-lo-sha mi yo-dei-ah? Sh'-lo-sha a-ni yo-dei-ah.
Sh'lo-sha a-vot. Sh'nei . . . (etc.)
4. Ar'-bah mi yo-dei-ah? Ar'-bah a-ni yo-dei-ah.
Ar'-bah i-ma-hot. Sh'-lo-sha . . .
5. Ḥa-mi-sha mi yo-dei-ah? Ha-mi-sha a-ni yo-dei-ah.
Ḥa-mi-sha ḥum-shei to-rah. Ar'-bah . . .
6. Shi-sha mi yo-dei-ah? Shi-sha a-ni yo-dei-ah.
Shi-sha sid-rei mish-na. Ḥa-mi-sha . . .
7. Shi-va mi yo-dei-ah? Shi-va a-ni yo-dei-ah.
Shi-va y'mei shab-ta. Shi-sha . . .
8. Sh'mo-na mi yo-dei-ah? Sh'mo-na a-ni yo-dei-ah.
Sh'mo-na y'-mei mi-lah. Shi-va . . .
9. Ti-sha mi yo-dei-ah? Ti-sha a-ni yo-dei-ah.
Ti-sha yar-ḥei lei-dah. Sh'mo-na . . .
10. A-sa-rah mi yo-dei-ah? A-sa-rah a-ni yo-dei-ah.
A-sa-rah dib'ra-yah. Ti-sha . . .
11. A-ḥad a-sar mi yo-dei-ah? A-ḥad a-sar a-ni yo-dei-ah.
A-ḥad a-sar koh-va-yah. A-sa-rah . . .
12. Sh'-neim a-sar mi yo-dei-ah? Sh'-neim a-sar a-ni yo-dei-ah.
Sh'-neim a-sar shiv-ta-yah. A-ḥad a-sar . . .
13. Sh'lo-sha a-sar mi yo-dei-ah? Sh'lo-sha a-sar a-ni yo-dei-ah.
Sh'lo-sha a-sar mi-da-yah.

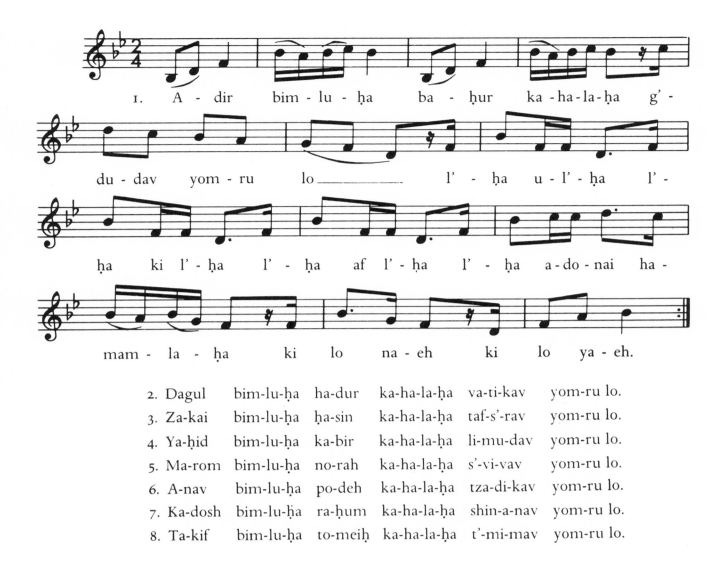

1. A - dir bim - lu - ḥa ba - ḥur ka - ha - la - ḥa g' -
du - dav yom - ru lo ______ l' - ḥa u - l' - ḥa l' -
ḥa ki l' - ḥa l' - ḥa af l' - ḥa l' - ḥa a - do - nai ha -
mam - la - ḥa ki lo na - eh ki lo ya - eh.

2. Dagul bim-lu-ḥa ha-dur ka-ha-la-ḥa va-ti-kav yom-ru lo.
3. Za-kai bim-lu-ḥa ḥa-sin ka-ha-la-ḥa taf-s'-rav yom-ru lo.
4. Ya-ḥid bim-lu-ḥa ka-bir ka-ha-la-ḥa li-mu-dav yom-ru lo.
5. Ma-rom bim-lu-ḥa no-rah ka-ha-la-ḥa s'-vi-vav yom-ru lo.
6. A-nav bim-lu-ḥa po-deh ka-ha-la-ḥa tza-di-kav yom-ru lo.
7. Ka-dosh bim-lu-ḥa ra-ḥum ka-ha-la-ḥa shin-a-nav yom-ru lo.
8. Ta-kif bim-lu-ḥa to-meiḥ ka-ha-la-ḥa t'-mi-mav yom-ru lo.

29 ḤAD GADYA

5. V'-a-tah nu-rah v'sa-raf l'ḥu-trah.
d'hi-kah l'ḥal-bah d'na-shaḥ l'shun-rah,
d'a-ḥal l'gad-ya di-z'van a-bah bit-rei zuzei . . .

6. V'-a-tah ma-yah v'ḥa-vah l'nu-rah,
d'sa-raf l'ḥu-trah d'hi-kah l'ḥal-bah,
d'na-shaḥ l'shun-rah d'a-ḥal l'gad-ya
di-z'van a-bah bit-rei zuzei . . .

7. V'-a-tah to-rah v'sha-tah l'ma-yah,
d'ḥa-vah l'nu-rah d'sa-raf l'ḥu-trah,
d'hi-kah l'ḥal-bah d'na-shaḥ l'shun-rah,
d'a-ḥal l'gad-ya di-z'van a-bah bit-rei zuzei . . .

8. V'-a-tah ha-sho-ḥeit v'sha-ḥat l'to-rah,
d'sha-tah l'ma-yah d'ḥa-vah l'nu-rah,
d'sa-raf l'ḥu-trah, d'hi-kah l'ḥal-bah,
d'na-shaḥ l'shun-rah d'a-ḥal l'gad-ya,
di-z'van a-bah bit-rei zuzei . . .

9. V'-a-tah mal-aḥ ha-ma-vet v'sha-ḥat la-sho-ḥeit,
d'sha-ḥat l'to-rah d'sha-tah l'ma-yah,
d'ḥa-vah l'nu-rah d'sa-raf l'ḥu-trah,
d'hi-kah l'ḥal-bah d'na-shaḥ l'shun-rah,
d'a-ḥal l'gad-ya di-z'van a-bah bit-rei zuzei . . .

30 KAREIV YOM

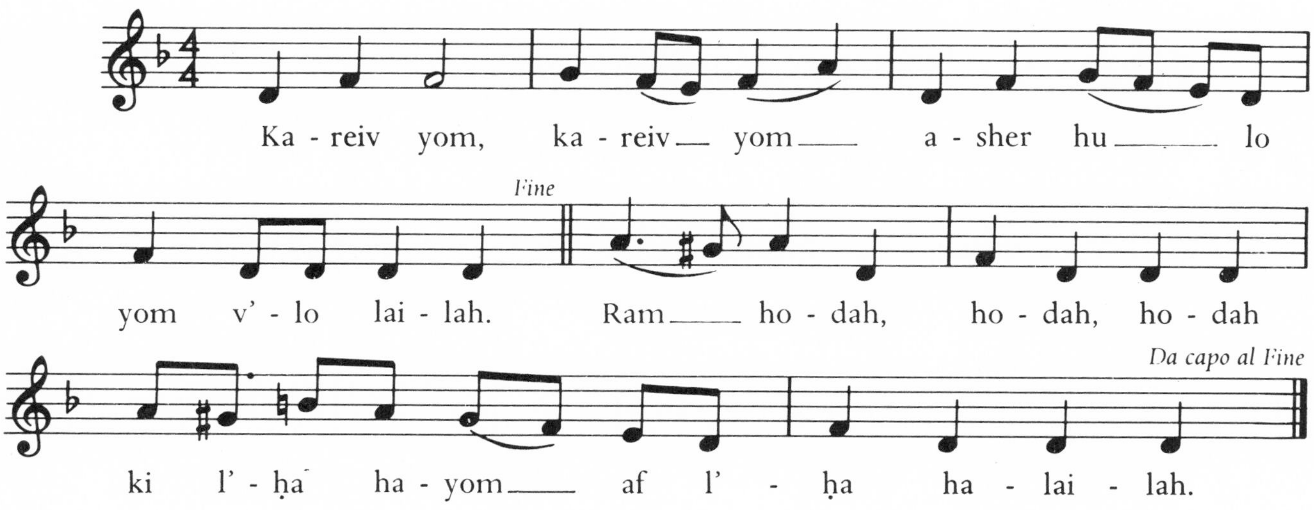
Fine
Da capo al Fine
Ka - reiv yom, ka - reiv yom a - sher hu lo
yom v' - lo lai - lah. Ram ho - dah, ho - dah, ho - dah
ki l' - ḥa ha - yom af l' - ḥa ha - lai - lah.

31 SAḤAKI

S. Chernichovsky

Adapted by H. Coopersmith

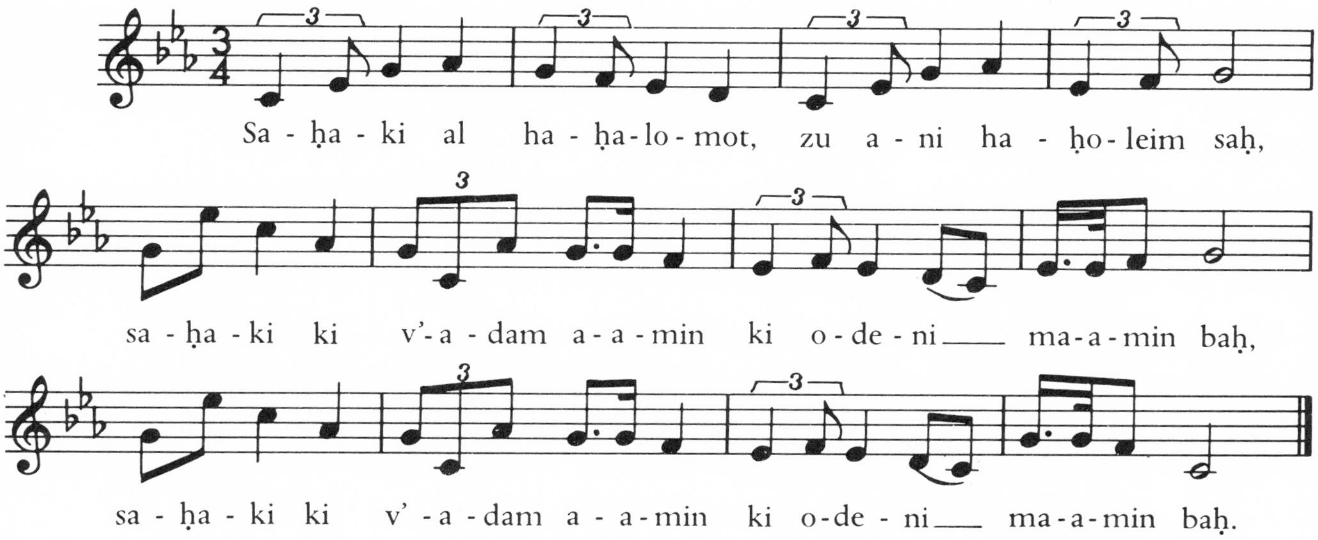
Sa - ḥa - ki al ha - ḥa - lo - mot, zu a - ni ha - ḥo - leim saḥ,
sa - ḥa - ki ki v'- a - dam a - a - min ki o - de - ni ma-a-min baḥ,
sa - ḥa - ki ki v' - a - dam a - a - min ki o-de - ni ma-a-min baḥ.

32 ḤASAL SIDUR PESAḤ

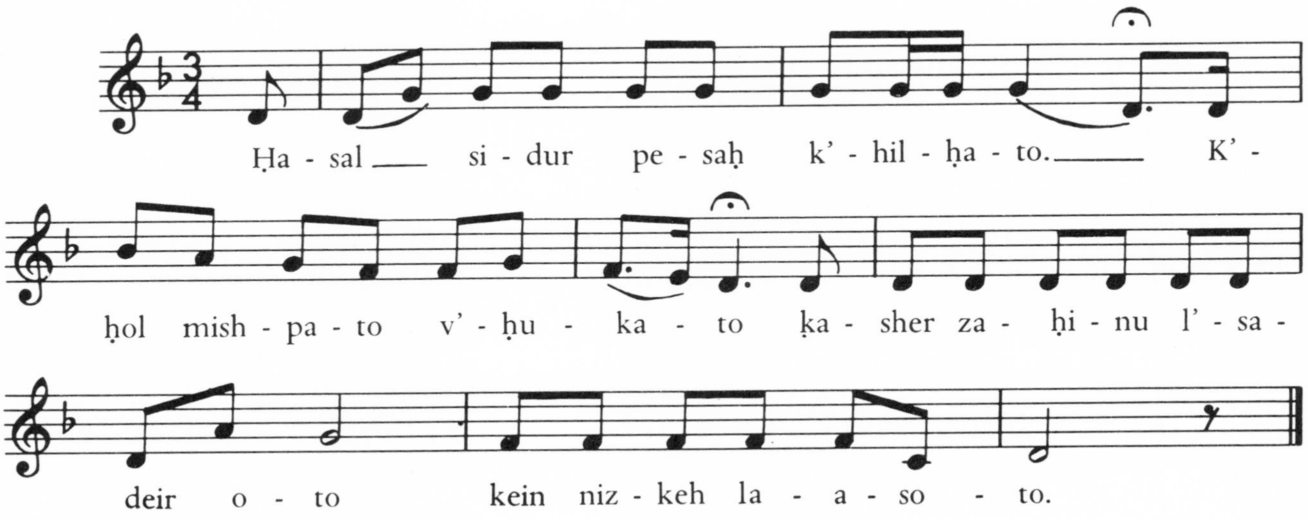
Ḥa - sal ___ si - dur pe - saḥ k' - hil - ḥa - to. ___ K' -
ḥol mish - pa - to v' - ḥu - ka - to ḳa - sher za - ḥi - nu l' - sa -
deir o - to kein niz - keh la - a - so - to.

33 L'SHANAH HABAAH

L' - sha - nah ha - ba - ah bi' - ru - sha - la - yim, l' - sha -
nah ha - ba - ah ___ bi' - ru - sha - la - yim, l' - sha - nah ha - ba - ah ___ bi' -
ru - sha - la - yim, l' - sha - nah ha - ba - ah bi' - ru - sha - la - yim.

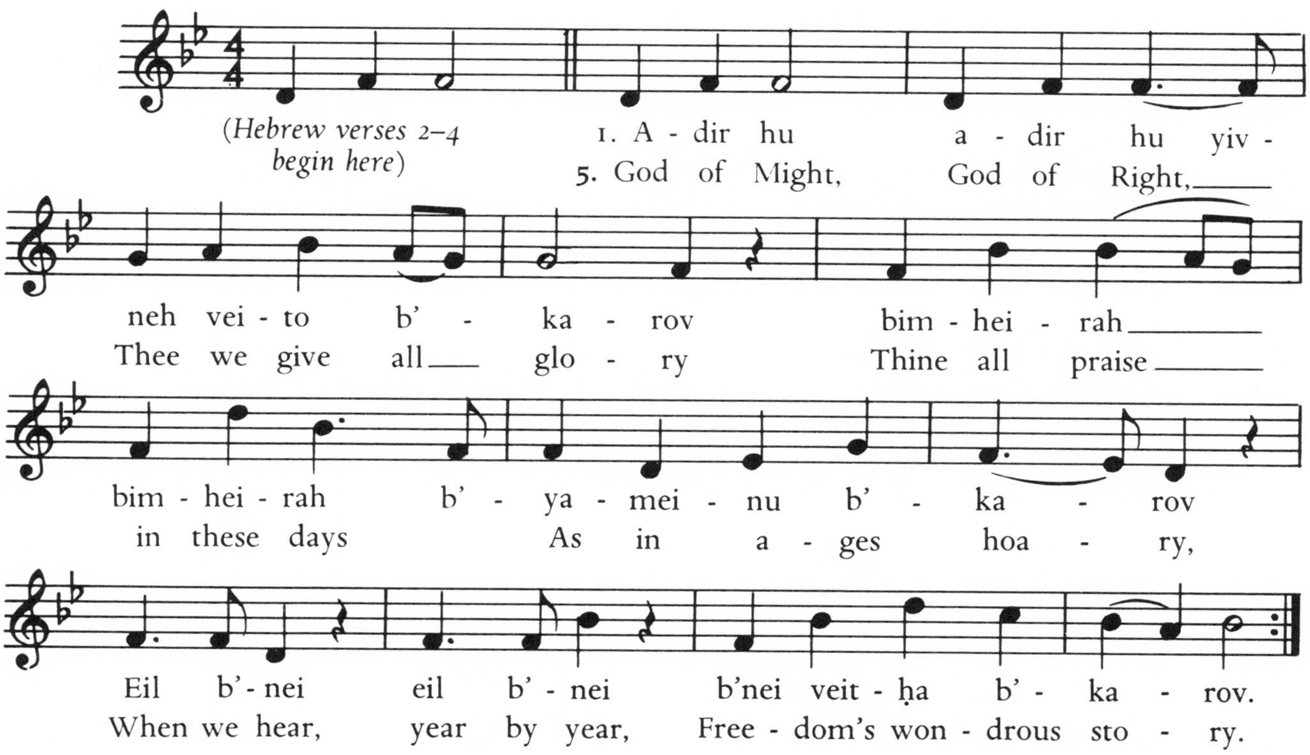
(Hebrew verses 2–4 begin here)
1. A - dir hu a - dir hu yiv - neh vei - to b' - ka - rov bim - hei - rah bim - hei - rah b' - ya - mei - nu b' - ka - rov Eil b' - nei eil b' - nei b'nei veit - ḥa b' - ka - rov.
5. God of Might, God of Right, Thee we give all glo - ry Thine all praise in these days As in a - ges hoa - ry, When we hear, year by year, Free - dom's won - drous sto - ry.

2. Ba-ḥur hu, ga-dol hu, da-gul hu . . .
3. Na-or hu, sa-giv hu, iz-uz hu . . .
4. Po-deh hu, tsa-dik hu, ka-dosh hu . . .

6. Now as erst, when Thou first
Mad'st the proclamation,
Warning loud ev'ry proud,
Ev'ry tyrant nation,
We Thy fame still proclaim
Bend in adoration.

7. Be with all who in thrall
To their task are driven;
In Thy power speed the hour
When their chains are riven;
Earth around will resound
Gleeful hymns to heaven.

(An alternate text)

1. God of Might, God of Right,
We would bow before Thee,
Sing Thy praise in these days,
Celebrate Thy glory,
As we hear, year by year,
Freedom's wondrous story:

2. How God gave to each slave
Promised liberation,
This great word Pharaoh heard
Making proclamation:
Set them free to serve Me
As a holy nation.

3. We enslaved thus were saved
Through God's might appearing,
So we pray for the day
When we shall be hearing
Freedom's call reaching all,
Mankind God revering.

ACKNOWLEDGMENTS

Acum Ltd.: *Avadim Hayinu* by S. Postolsky, © by Hamerkaz Letarbut Ulechinuch, Musical Library, Tel-Aviv.

Behrman House, Inc.: "Babylonian Melody" by Judith Eisenstein from *The Gateway to Jewish Song.*

Bloch Publishing Company: From *Why I Am A Jew* by Edmond Fleg.

The Brandeis Institute: *Osay Shalom* by Helfman.

Doubleday & Company, Inc.: From *Anne Frank: The Diary of a Young Girl* by Anne Frank, Copyright 1952 by Otto H. Frank. Reprinted by permission of Doubleday & Company, Inc.

Judith K. Eisenstein: "Babylonian Melody" from *The Gateway to Jewish Song.*

Farrar, Straus & Giroux, Inc.: From *The Sabbath* by Abraham Joshua Heschel. Copyright 1951 by Abraham Joshua Heschel. Reprinted by permission of Farrar, Straus, & Giroux, Inc.

Friends of Jewish Music: "Kindling The Lights" from *The Congregation Sings.*

Hebrew Publishing Company: "Birkat Hamazon" from *Rabotai Nevarech* by M. Nathanson.

Holt, Rinehart and Winston, Inc.: From *Freedom Seder* by Arthur I. Waskow. Copyright © 1969, 1970 by The Religious Community of Micah.

From "Poem—1959" by Samuel Halkin, translated by Edwin Honig, from *A Treasury of Yiddish Poetry* edited by Irving Howe and Eliezer Greenberg. Copyright © 1969 by Irving Howe and Eliezer Greenberg. Reprinted by permission of Holt, Rinehart and Winston, Inc.

The Jewish Publication Society of America: From *The Legends of the Jews* by Louis Ginzberg.

McGraw-Hill Book Company: From *. . . I Never Saw Another Butterfly . . .* edited by N. Volavkova, 1964. McGraw-Hill Book Company. Used with permission.

Philosophical Library, Inc., and the Estate of Albert Einstein: From *Out of My Later Years* by Albert Einstein.

Random House, Inc.: From *One Generation After* by Elie Wiesel. Copyright © 1965, 1967, 1970 by Elie Wiesel.

Reconstructionist Press: "Vay'hulu" from *What Is Torah?*

Mrs. Maurice Samuel: "Credo" by Saul Chernichovsky, and "The Dead of the Wilderness," by Hayim Nachman Bialik, translated by Maurice Samuel.

Schocken Books Inc.: From *Tales of the Hasidim: The Early Masters* by Martin Buber. Copyright © 1947 by Schocken Books Inc.

University of California Press: From *Modern Hebrew Poetry: A Bilingual Anthology*, edited and translated by Ruth Finer Mintz, University of California Press, 1966.

The text for this Haggadah was set by
the press of Maurice Jacobs, Inc., Philadelphia.
The English text is Dante, a monotype face
designed by Giovanni Mardersteig.
The Hebrew is Peninim 217M with Soncino.
The color illustrations were reproduced by
Litho Art, Inc., New York.
This book was printed and bound by
Kingsport Press, Inc., Kingsport, Tennessee.
Designed by Leonard Baskin,
with Jacqueline Schuman.

D1222407